ROBERT GARDNER'S FAVORITE SCIENCE EXPERIMENTS

ROBERT GARDNER'S FAVORITE SCIENCE EXPERIMENTS

by ROBERT GARDNER

FRANKLIN WATTS
NEW YORK/CHICAGO/LONDON/TORONTO/SYDNEY

To the memory of David Webster,
whose support and encouragement
led me to become a writer.

Photographs copyright ©: Educational Development Center
Inc.: p. 48; PHOTRI Inc.: pp. 50 (Tom Sanders), 105; Photo
Researchers/Barbara Rios: p. 73; NASA: p. 86; Terence
Dickinson: p. 95; Alaska Division of Tourism: p. 118.
All other photographs courtesy of the author.

Diagrams by Vantage Art, Inc.

Library of Congress Cataloging-in-Publication Data

Gardner, Robert, 1929–
[Favorite science experiments]
Robert Gardner's favorite science experiments /
by Robert Gardner.
p.   cm.
Includes bibliographical references and index.
Summary: Science experiments, mostly using materials
found in the home, demonstrating principles of chemistry,
mechanics, biology, light, astronomy, heat, and electricity.
ISBN 0-531-11038-9 (lib.). — ISBN 0-531-15255-3 (pbk.)
1. Science—Experiments—Juvenile literature.
[1. Science—Experiments.   2. Experiments.]   I. Title.
II. Title: Favorite science experiments.
Q164.G32   1992
507.8—dc20   92-17579   CIP   AC

CONTENTS

TO THE READER

I was delighted when Franklin Watts asked me to write a book of my favorite experiments. After all, few authors and teachers have the opportunity to review and cull what they have done over many years. On the other hand, reviewing all that I have written, taught, and read has made me realize that I spent a great many years teaching, writing, and reading science. And while you may find it hard to believe at your age, most adults don't enjoy growing older. Nevertheless, I regard the opportunity to write this book as one of the privileges of having lived and worked a long time. I hope you will enjoy reading it and doing the experiments as much as I have enjoyed writing it.

To make things easier for you, I have included a list of the things you'll need to do each experiment. Most of these materials you can find in your home. If you have to buy anything, it won't be very expensive. A few things you may be able to borrow from your science teacher. On occasion, for reasons of safety, you should ask an adult to help you.

Before each experiment, I've explained why I like it or what is special about it. This often involves telling you what *I* hope you'll learn from it. It may not be the same reason *you* like the experiment. Of course, if you don't like the experiment, you don't have to do it. But do me a favor. At least read why I've included it. Maybe then you'll see it's worth doing even if at first you don't like it.

—R. G.

1

EXPERIMENTS WITH CHEMICAL PROPERTIES AND CHANGES

A chemical reaction occurs when substances change their identity. New substances form from other substances that disappear. It's surprising how much chemistry you can do in your own home. A pantry, kitchen cabinet, and medicine chest contain a variety of substances that can be used for chemical reactions. The first experiment involves solutions. Now in a solution, substances disappear but new substances do not appear so it is not a chemical reaction. In fact, we can get back the substance that disappeared and see that it is unchanged. Solutions are introduced first because they are necessary for some of the experiments that follow.

The second experiment is not a chemical reaction either. But density—the compactness of matter—is such a basic property that everyone should understand it. The idea of density is used not only in chemistry but in physics, biology, and every branch of science and social science.

The third experiment reveals how strongly the molecules of water attract one another, and the fourth makes use of water's properties to separate the chemicals in ink and food coloring. The re-

9

maining experiments involve chemical reactions that can be done with materials found mostly in your kitchen or bathroom.

<table>
<tr><td>

DISAPPEARING ACTS

When a solid is stirred in a liquid, it sometimes disappears. When it does, we say the solid has *dissolved* to form a *solution*. This experiment makes it clear that some substances will dissolve and others will not. It also reveals that solutions are not limited to solids dissolved in liquids. Gases can dissolve in liquids and so can other liquids. Similarly, liquids can dissolve in gases and gases can dissolve in other gases.

</td><td>

Things You'll Need

- water
- several small jars such as baby food jars or test tubes
- teaspoon
- solids—salt, sugar, flour
- liquids—rubbing alcohol, cooking oil
- bottle of Coke or Pepsi
- balloon
- ice cubes
- shiny tin can

</td></tr>
</table>

Pour about 20 mL of water into each of three small jars or test tubes. To the first jar or test tube add about ¼ teaspoonful of salt. Add the same amount of sugar to the second, and the same amount of flour to the third. Stir or shake the mixtures. Which of the solids disappear in water? Which one does not?

Can you dissolve more of the soluble solids? To find out, add another ¼ teaspoonful of each and stir or shake. When no more solid will dissolve, the solution is said to be *saturated*. How much of each solid is needed to make a saturated solution?

Now add a few drops of rubbing alcohol to a jar or test tube of water and shake. Is the alcohol soluble in water? Try adding cooking oil to water.

Is cooking oil soluble in water? How do you know?

Gases can also dissolve in liquids. To see that this is true, open a bottle of Coke or Pepsi. Slip the neck of a balloon over the top of the bottle and swirl. What happens to the balloon? How can you explain what you see?

You may have been surprised to learn that liquids can evaporate and dissolve in gases. Watch what happens to the water dissolved in air when the air is cooled. Place some ice cubes in the shiny can. Watch for water droplets to form on the outside of the can as the air is cooled when it strikes the cold container. You've probably seen the same thing on a pitcher of cold milk or iced tea in the summertime.

DENSITY

The density of an object is a measurement of its "heaviness," that is, how much a unit volume of the object weighs. Measuring the density of something is a straightforward experiment. You simply find the object's weight and volume. Then you divide the weight by the volume to find the weight per volume. For example, if an object's mass is 200 g (grams) and its volume is 20 milliliters (mL), its density is 200g/20 mL = 10g/mL. The idea of density is used in a variety of ways. You may have heard of population density, the number of people per square mile, or "dense" underbrush, which simply means lots of bushes per area. An understanding of density will help you to grasp a variety of ideas that you'll encounter. Among other things, it will help you to explain why some things float and others sink.

Things You'll Need

- balance or scale to weigh things
- medicine cup, measuring cup, or graduated cylinder
- water
- cooking oil
- soda straw
- drinking glasses
- clay or Plasticine

Use the balance or scale to weigh an empty medicine cup, measuring cup, or graduated cylinder. Then fill the cup or cylinder to the 30-mL, or 1-oz (ounce), mark with water. Reweigh the container with the water in it. Subtract the weight of the cup or cylinder from the total weight of the container and water to find the weight of the water. How much does 30 mL (1 oz) of water weigh? What is the density of water according to your measurements?

Repeat the experiment using cooking oil in place of water. What is the density of cooking oil?

Remove some cooking oil from its container by lowering a straw into the oil as shown in Figure 1. Insert the straw into the container. Place your finger firmly against the top of the straw. If you keep your finger over the top, you'll be able to lift the straw with the oil in it. Now hold the straw so its lower end is just touching the surface of some water in the glass. If you remove your finger, do you think the oil will sink to the bottom or float on top of the water? What happens when you do remove your finger? Was your prediction right?

Repeat the experiment, but this time place the straw with the cooking oil deeper into the water. Be sure the level of the cooking oil in the straw is lower than the water outside the straw. What do you think will happen this time when you remove your finger? Were you right? Can you pick up a two-layered liquid with the straw?

What does this experiment tell you about the relationship between density and floating?

If you drop a piece of clay into some water, does it sink or float? Do you think clay is more or

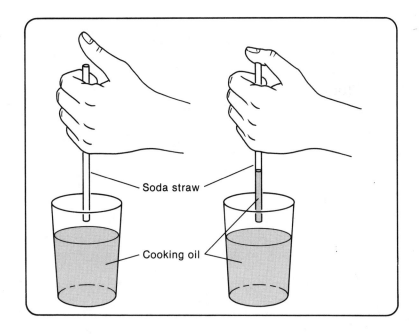

Figure 1. Picking up cooking oil with a soda straw

less dense than water? What can you do to find out? What is the density of clay? What can you do to make the clay float in water?

HEAPING AND WATER'S "SKIN"

You may never have thought about water as being "sticky," but when you see water behave as it does here, you'll know for certain that water "holds together" very well. Although water doesn't really have a skin, it certainly behaves as if it does. Water molecules attract one another so strongly that the surface of water will bend and stretch to support an object that will sink once it breaks the water's skin.

Things You'll Need

- medicine cup or pill vial
- eyedropper and water
- medicine cup or graduated cylinder
- dinner fork
- large dish
- rubbing alcohol

Notice that large straps have been used to fasten this oil tank, which is about to be buried in wet soil, to a concrete slab. If the tank were not fastened, what would happen in very rainy weather when the soil became filled with water? (Hint: Think about what you have learned about density.)

Fill the medicine cup or the pill vial nearly full of water. Then use the eyedropper to add water drop by drop to the cup or vial. How much water can you add before it overflows? Does the water level rise above the top of the cup or vial?

Repeat the experiment. This time add water to the container until the water level is even with the top. Then count the number of drops that you can add before water spills out. How many drops did you add?

To find out what volume of water you added, find out how many drops it takes to fill a graduated (one with volume marks on the side) medicine cup or measuring cup to the 10-mL or $\frac{1}{2}$-oz line. Suppose it takes 200 drops to reach the 10-mL line. Then each drop is $\frac{1}{20}$ mL (10 mL/200). What volume of water were you able to add to the cup or vial after it was "full."

For more evidence of water's skin, use the fork to gently place a paper clip on the surface of some water in a large dish. You'll find that the paper clip will stay on top of the water. If you look closely at the surface around the paper clip, you'll see that the water's skin is "stretched." What would happen if you were to push the paper clip beneath the surface?

An Extension: Try heaping rubbing alcohol or soapy water in the same cup or vial you used for water. How much alcohol or soapy water can you heap above the top? Do you think drops of alcohol or soapy water will be larger or smaller than water drops? How can you test your prediction?

This paper clip is floating on water. What would happen if you touched the water with a bar of soap?

HIDDEN RAINBOWS

I think most people enjoy colorful experiments, and this experiment is colorful, even when you use black ink. It's another experiment that shows how well water holds together, but it also reveals that some inks are made up of several dyes. As these dyes are carried upward by the water in which they dissolve, some move faster than others. After a while they become separated. This experiment is an example of *chromatography*, which is used by chemists to separate the substances found in a mixture.

Things You'll Need

- scissors
- coffee filters or white blotter paper
- magnifying glass or microscope
- several kinds of black pens
- toothpicks
- several food colors
- water
- shallow, wide container
- tall bottles or jars and aluminum foil
- rubbing alcohol

Use the scissors to cut some strips about 6 inches (15 cm) long and 1 inch (2 cm) wide from a coffee filter or a sheet of white blotter paper. Look at these paper strips with a magnifying glass or a microscope. You'll see that they consist of tiny wood fibers that are very close together. Water is attracted to the fibers and so it will "climb" up through the tiny spaces between the fibers. But water molecules also attract one another. The molecules that are pulled up into the spaces by their attraction for the wood will pull other water molecules along with them. This will go on until the weight of the water balances its attraction for the wood.

If the water moves over substances that will dissolve in it, they will be carried upward along with the water. However, if there are several substances, some will be dragged along faster than others. In this experiment you'll use black ink and food coloring to see if they are mixtures that can be separated by chromatography.

Draw a narrow line with one of the black pens about half an inch (1 cm) from one end of a strip. Repeat the procedure for each pen on separate strips. See Figure 2a. Then draw similar lines using toothpicks dipped in each of the food colors you want to test. The lower ends of the strips, below where the lines have been drawn, should just touch the surface of the water in the wide container. Use tape to fasten the upper ends of the strips to a stick or rod fastened to a cabinet, table, or chair.

Figure 2. Separating dyes by chromatography.
A) In air B) In a closed container

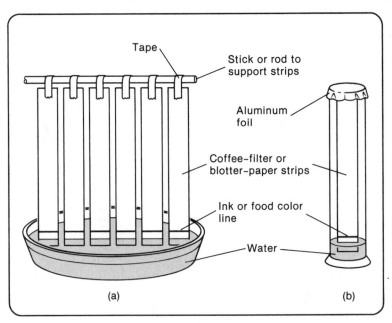

Watch the water move up the strips. What happens when the water reaches the black or colored lines? Leave the strips for an hour or so. If the air is very dry, the water may not carry the dyes in the ink far enough to separate them. If that is the case, support the strips in tall bottles or jars covered with aluminum foil as shown in Figure 2b. This will reduce the evaporation rate so that the water will travel farther up the strip.

Do any of the inks contain more than one dye? Do any of the food colors contain more than one dye? How can you tell if the inks are different? How can you tell how many dyes are in each of the food colors?

If you use an ink that's not soluble in water, it won't move up the strip. In that case, try using rubbing alcohol in place of water. **Do not use alcohol near a flame! It is flammable.** Because alcohol evaporates faster than water, you'll want to use a bottle or a jar to enclose the paper strip.

A CHEMICAL REACTION: FAST AND SLOW

In this experiment you see a chemical reaction—a change in which at least one new kind of matter is formed. In this experiment the new matter is a gas. The bubbles that form clearly reveal its presence. The reaction is a common one and one that is easily performed. But I like it because it's a good one for showing how the speed of a chemical reaction can be changed.

Things You'll Need

- seltzer tablets
- two drinking glasses
- tap water, cold and hot

Drop a seltzer tablet into a glass of water. What evidence do you have that a chemical reaction is taking place? Now repeat the experiment with two glasses of water. The water in one glass should be hot; the water in the other glass should be cold. Drop a seltzer tablet into each glass at the same time. In which glass of water is the reaction faster? How do you know?

Next, crush one seltzer tablet into tiny pieces on a small sheet of paper; leave a second tablet whole. As you can see, the crushed tablet has a lot more surface exposed than the whole tablet. By crushing it, seltzer that was inside the tablet before is now exposed and visible. The surface area of the seltzer in contact with the air has increased.

Let the crushed tablet slide off the paper into a glass of cold water. At the same time, have a friend drop the whole tablet into a second glass that contains the same amount of water at the same temperature. How does the amount of surface area affect the speed of this reaction?

BAKING POWDER: THE BAKER'S "FRIEND"	Things You'll Need
Chemical reactions often accompany cooking. In this experiment, you'll "bake" two very small and simple loaves of bread. The ingredients of the second loaf include a substance not used with the first loaf, and the results will be different. By carrying out a second experiment, you'll see what the effect of the added ingredient is. Then you should be able to see why the loaves turned out as they did. I like this experiment because it shows you how a chemical reaction is involved in baking, a very common activity.	• teaspoon • flour • small dish • water • baking powder • small frying pan • margarine, butter, or lard • stove • spatula • small jar or test tube

To make the dough for your first loaf of bread add 3 teaspoonfuls of the flour to a small dish.

Add enough water to make the flour stick together like a paste. Make the second loaf by mixing 3 teaspoonfuls of flour with 1 teaspoonful of baking powder. Again, add enough water to make a paste-like dough. Cover the bottom of a small frying pan with a little margarine, butter, or lard. Place the loaves you have prepared in the pan. **With an adult present,** place the pan on a stove burner and heat slowly. What happens to the two loaves as they get warm? **Under adult supervision,** after they become firmer you may want to turn them with the spatula. In that way they will be heated on all sides.

When you think the loaves are done, turn off the stove and wait for the bread to cool. Then put the loaves on a paper towel and examine them. As you can see, the bread without the baking soda is more dense than the loaf that contained baking powder. How can you tell that it is more dense?

Now break open the two loaves. How do their textures compare? You can probably see that there are openings or holes inside the bread that contained baking powder. It looks as though a gas was produced as the bread cooked. In which loaf did a chemical reaction take place? Which loaf would you prefer to eat? Go ahead and perform a taste test.

Place a teaspoonful of baking powder in a small jar or test tube and add some water. Do you see any evidence that a gas is produced? Hold your ear near the jar or tube. Can you hear any fizzing?

As you have seen, baking powder reacts with water to form a gas. Baking powder and baking soda both release a gas when they are heated.

Why do bakers often add baking powder or baking soda to flour?

ACIDS AND BASES

Acids and bases are a vital part of chemistry. People tend to think of acids as substances that can "eat away" your flesh, and, indeed, some acids can. There are other acids, however, such as the citric acid in citrus fruit or the acetic acid in vinegar, that add zest to food. Bases include such substances as lye, which is used to make soap and clean out drains, and ammonia, which dissolved in water, is a common household cleaner.

Certain chemicals such as litmus, grape juice, the juices in red cabbage leaves, and a number of other substances turn one color in a base and another color in an acid. These substances are called acid-base indicators because they can indicate whether a substance is an acid, a base, or neither (a neutral substance). Phenolphthalein, which you will use in this experiment, is one such indicator. I chose phenolphthalein because it can also be used in a science "magic" trick that you may enjoy.

Things You'll Need

- laxative tablets that contain phenolphthalein
- paper
- spoon
- small jars, vials, or test tubes
- rubbing alcohol
- two or more eyedroppers
- household ammonia
- vinegar
- soda straw
- juices—lemon, apple, grapefruit
- solids dissolved in water—cleansing powder, salt, sugar, aspirin, wood ashes, baking soda, baking powder, Kool-Aid crystals, washing soda
- litmus paper (optional)

Your school may have a solution of phenolphthalein, but you can make your own. Many laxative tablets contain phenolphthalein. Look for the name among the ingredients listed on the package. Place a laxative tablet that contains this chemical on a small sheet of paper. Use the back of a spoon to crush the tablet into a fine powder. Pour the powder into a small jar such as a baby food jar and add about 20 mL of rubbing alcohol. Stir the mixture thoroughly to dissolve as much of the powder as possible; then let it settle. Pour off the liquid into another jar.

Use an eyedropper to add several drops of the phenolphthalein solution to a few milliliters of the ammonia solution. What color suddenly appears? What is the color of phenolphthalein in a base? Repeat the experiment using vinegar in place of ammonia. You'll notice that phenolphthalein remains clear in an acid such as vinegar.

What do you think will happen if you add ammonia to the vinegar that contains phenolphthalein? To find out, use a different eyedropper, one that has not been in phenolphthalein. Add ammonia drop by drop to the vinegar as you stir the mixture with a soda straw. What happens? Was it what you predicted?

The process of adding an acid to a base, or a base to an acid, can result in a neutral solution, one that is neither acidic nor basic. Indicators can be used to show when just enough of one substance has been added to neutralize the other. As you saw, a single drop of ammonia was enough to change the color of phenolphthalein in vinegar from colorless to red.

Use drops of the phenolphthalein solution you made, or strips of litmus paper, to find out whether each of the following is an acid, a base, or a neutral substance. If you can't tell whether something is neutral or acidic using phenolphthalein, add a drop of the ammonia. If it turns red immediately, it must have been neutral. If it takes several drops, it must have been an acid and the color won't change until the acid is neutralized by the ammonia.

Test the following juices: lemon, apple, and grapefruit. Then test as many of the following solids as possible *after* they have been added to water in small jars, vials, or test tubes: cleanser powder, salt, sugar, aspirin, wood ashes, baking soda, baking powder, lime (calcium oxide), citric acid or Kool-Aid crystals, and washing soda. Which are acids? Which are bases? Which ones are neutral?

• Now here's a science magic trick you can do using ammonia and the phenolphthalein you made.

Tell some friends that you have made a fluid that protects your hands from strong acids. Then place a drop or two of the phenolphthalein solution you made on the palm of your hand. Use the fingers of your other hand to spread the liquid over the center of your palm. Then tell your friends that you're going to add a drop of strong acid to your hand to show them how good your protective fluid is.

You then add a drop of ammonia, which they think is the acid, to your hand. You look in mock horror at your hand and hold it up for them to see saying, "I've made a terrible mistake!" Your palm has turned red, of course, which they will think is blood.

Then, before they become too concerned, wipe away the liquid with a paper towel and assure them that you're okay.

PHENOLPHTHALEIN: AN INVISIBLE INK

The same acid-base indicator, phenolphthalein, can be used as an invisible ink. It's always fascinating to see letters or words appear as if by magic from a blank sheet of paper. As any magician will tell you, a magic show consists of a series of clever tricks. Once you understand how the trick is done, you realize there is no magic. You may marvel at the magician's sleight of hand, his or her ability to divert the audience's attention, or to devise the apparatus used in the trick—but you know it's a trick. There is no magic. Understanding that the letters written with "invisible ink" appear because of a chemical reaction will help you to understand that there are logical explanations for things that may appear to be magic.

Things You'll Need

- phenolphthalein solution prepared in the previous experiment
- toothpick
- white paper
- household ammonia
- drinking glass, beaker, or shallow dish

You can use the solution of phenolphthalein that you prepared in the previous experiment as an invisible ink. The end of a toothpick can serve as a pen. Use your toothpick pen and the phenolphthalein invisible ink to write a message or someone's initials on a blank sheet of white paper. Once the "ink" has dried, you can use a "magic solution" to make the letters appear. The magic solution, as you might guess, is household ammonia. Pour the ammonia solution into a glass or beaker. Then place the blank sheet of paper, message side down, over the glass, beaker, or dish. The ammonia fumes will react with the phenolphthalein indicator producing a pink-colored message or pink initials.

HOW MUCH OF THE AIR IS OXYGEN?

You've probably heard that air is mainly a mixture of nitrogen and oxygen. This experiment enables you to find out what fraction of the air is oxygen. At the same time, you will see the effect of a catalyst. A catalyst is a substance that changes the rate of a chemical reaction without being changed itself.

Things You'll Need

- pad of *soapless* steel wool
- drinking glass
- vinegar
- paper towels
- tall, narrow jar such as an olive jar
- shallow pan of water
- marking pen
- ruler

Pull a few strands from the pad of steel wool, and roll them into two small, loose balls. Dip one of the steel wool balls into a glass of vinegar. Then place both samples of steel wool on a paper towel. Label the ball that was dipped in vinegar. Watch the two steel wool balls over the next 24 hours. Which ball rusts faster? You can identify the rust. It is the dark-red material that forms on the steel. It may also fall onto and stain the paper towel. The rust, which is iron oxide, forms when iron (in the steel) combines with oxygen in the air.

Now that you know how to make iron rust fast using vinegar as a catalyst, you can use that reaction to find out what fraction of the air is oxygen. Push a small ball of steel wool into a glass of vinegar. After several minutes, remove the steel wool ball and push it to the bottom of a tall, narrow jar such as the kind olives come in. Turn the jar upside down and place it in the shallow pan of water. Air is now trapped in the jar. See Figure 3. As the iron combines with the oxygen in

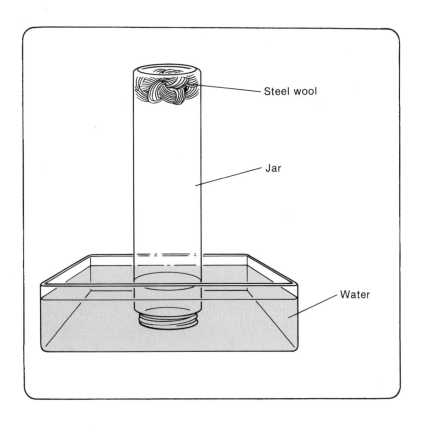

Figure 3. How much of the air is oxygen?

the air, water will enter the jar to replace the oxygen. Watch the reaction over a period of a day. You'll see the water rise slowly in the jar.

When the water stops rising, use a pen to make a mark at the level of the water. Remove the jar and use a ruler to measure the total height of the jar. Then measure the height to which the water rose. What fraction of the air was oxygen according to your measurements?

2

EXPERIMENTS WITH MECHANICAL THINGS

In this chapter you'll experiment with mechanical things—boats, swings, seesaws, slides, whirligigs, toy cars, wheels, towers, and paper airplanes. Along the way, you'll learn more about science and how it works.

You'll find out that changing one thing, such as the length of a pendulum, can sometimes change something else, such as the time for the pendulum to swing back and forth. On the other hand, changing other things, such as the weight of the pendulum bob, may have no effect on the swing time.

You'll see how frictional forces make you work harder or reduce the rate at which an object falls. And you'll also learn ways to reduce friction and thereby make work easier.

During World War II, the United States built a number of boats that were made of concrete. Before you say "But that's impossible!", think about all the steel boats that are afloat on the world's oceans.

This experiment is related to the one you did on density in Chapter 1. It's true that objects more dense than water will sink in that liquid. But you can build an object in such a way that it encloses a lot of empty space. Then the density of the whole object will be less than the density of the material it's made of. You'll see how this works by building some boats of your own.

- piece of wood
- small piece of *new* aluminum foil
- clay or Plasticine
- steel washers
- large pan of lukewarm water
- empty tuna fish can
- cargo—small steel washers, pennies, or marbles

Drop a piece of wood, a lump of clay or Plasticine, a steel washer, and a small piece of *new* aluminum foil that you've folded and pressed into a small square into a pan of lukewarm water. Do any of these objects float? Which material would you feel confident about using if you were going to build a boat?

You're probably sure you could build a boat from wood because it floats. But is it possible to make a boat from materials that sink in water? Begin by folding a piece of aluminum foil into a boatlike shape. Will your aluminum boat float on water?

You can make a simple round steel boat from an empty tuna fish can. Will this steel boat float?

Try building a boat from a piece of clay. Can you make a clay boat that will float in water? How much cargo will your boat hold without sinking? Your standard cargo might consist of small steel washers, pennies, or marbles. Can a bigger boat made with more clay hold more cargo?

Crumple a piece of aluminum foil into a small ball and drop it into water. When the folded piece of aluminum was dropped into water it sank. Why do you think the crumpled aluminum floats?

Now that you know how to make boats from aluminum, steel, and clay, how would go about building a concrete boat?

PLAYGROUND PHYSICS

The swing on a playground is a kind of pendulum, like the pendulum that swings back and forth on a grandfather's clock. The seesaw is similar to a balance used to weigh things in a chemistry laboratory. A slide is similar to the inclined plane used when heavy objects have to be wheeled onto a truck. And a whirligig, a giant lazy Susan like the one in Figure 4, has certain properties like a centrifuge's. It can be used to demonstrate what Sir Isaac Newton called the first law of motion: a body will keep moving in the same direction with the same speed unless a force (a push or pull) is applied to it.

One of the nice things about these playground experiments is that they can be used to show how one variable may or may not affect another variable. A variable is something that can change. For example, a playground swing can be made longer or shorter. The weight on the swing can be made bigger or smaller depending on who sits on it. How does changing each of these variables affect the period of the swing, that is, the time it takes for the swing to make one round trip (over and back)? You can find out by doing this experiment.

Things You'll Need

- playground swings of different lengths
- stopwatch or watch with a second hand
- seesaw (teeter-totter)
- playground whirligig
- a ball, such as a tennis ball
- cardboard, different types of cloth, newspaper, plastic wrap, aluminum foil, sandpaper

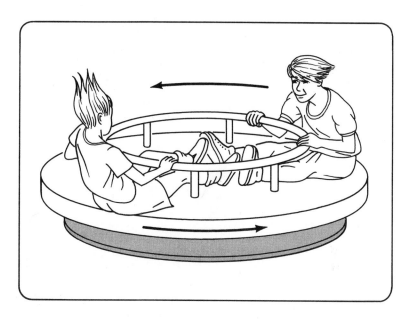

Figure 4. A playground whirligig or whirlaround like this one can be used to investigate motion.

Sit on a playground swing. Have someone give you a little push so that you swing back and forth through a small arc. Now have someone with a stopwatch or a watch with a second hand measure the time it takes for you to make 30 complete swings, that is, 30 round trips over and back. Remember, you have to go over and back once *before* you count 1. The starting time is 0! The person should start timing when you are at one end of your swing. At that point he or she calls out "Zero!" After you have counted 30 swings, call out "Time!" At that moment your timer stops the watch or notes the number of seconds that have passed.

The time to make just one round trip is called the period of the swing. To find the period just divide the total time it took to make 30 swings by 30. For example, if it took 84 seconds to make 30 complete swings, then the period is

$$\frac{84 \text{ s}}{30} = 2\frac{24}{30} \text{ s} = 2\frac{8}{10} \text{ s or 2.8 s.}$$

What happens to the period or the time to make 30 complete swings if you swing through a larger arc? Try it. Does the period get longer, shorter, or stay about the same? What happens to the period if a heavier person sits on the swing? A lighter person?

As you've seen, the length of the arc and the weight of the person have little, if any, effect on the period of the swing. But suppose you sit on a swing that is longer or shorter. See Figure 5. What happens to the period if the swing is longer? If the swing is shorter?

Sit on a seesaw and have a friend sit on the other side. If the seesaw is to balance, how must your friend's weight compare with yours? Suppose the person on the other side of the seesaw is an adult or someone much heavier than you. How can the seesaw be made to balance? How can it be made to balance if the person on the other side is someone much lighter than you?

Many people think that if you swing something in a circle and release it, it will fly outward. This is not true as any hammer thrower will tell you. To find the path followed by an object that is released when it is moving in a circle try this. Sit near the outside edge of a playground whirligig and have some one spin the whirligig. Ask an-

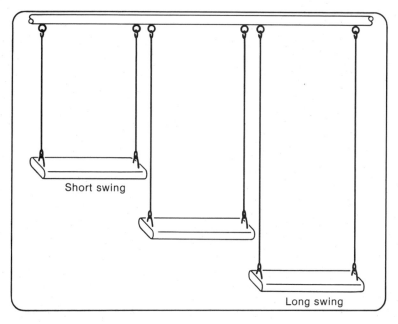

Figure 5. The length of a swing is a variable. It can change. Does the period of the swing depend on its length?

other person to stand near the spinning whirligig. Once you are turning at a comfortable speed, hold a ball, such as a tennis ball, just beyond the edge of the platform. At the moment you pass the person who is standing near the whirligig, drop the ball. Don't throw it; just release it. Have the person who is standing nearby watch the path of the ball. Does it bounce outward into that person or does it bounce along in the direction it was going when it was released?

To see for yourself that the ball continues in the direction it was moving when it was released, switch places with the person who stood beside the whirligig and repeat the experiment.

The playground slide is a good place to investigate friction. Try sitting on different things as you go down the slide. You might try pieces of cardboard, different types of cloth, newspaper, plastic wrap, aluminum foil, and sandpaper. On which material do you slide fastest? Slowest? The rate at which you slide depends on the friction between the slide and the material you're sitting on. Friction is the subject of my next favorite experiment.

FRICTION AND NO FRICTION

You know that if you try to slide a box along the floor, something continually pushes back against you. That something is a force called *friction*. It's a force that always exists when one surface rubs against another. Everyone talks about friction, but very few people know much about it. It's an interesting force because its properties can be surprising.

In this experiment you'll investigate some of the factors that affect friction. Then you'll examine some ways to decrease friction. Finally, you'll build an air-car that moves almost as if there were no friction, a condition we call frictionless. Actually, it's impossible to eliminate friction completely, but you'll come close with the air-car.

Things You'll Need

- three wood blocks about 3½ in × 3½ in × 1½ in
- smooth board about 8 in × 24 in
- ruler, yardstick, or meter stick
- toy truck, and spring balance or long, thin rubber band
- various surfaces for the blocks—wide rubber bands, thumbtacks, felt pads, aluminum foil, waxed paper, construction paper, etc.
- tools—saw, sandpaper, drill (¹/₁₆ in) and bit
- small piece of ¼-in plywood
- wood spool (empty spool of thread)
- balloon

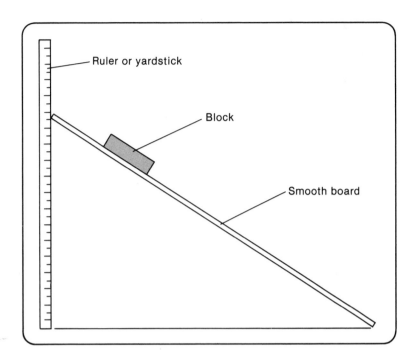

Figure 6. A way to compare the friction
of different surfaces

You know that it's much easier to walk along a
rubber mat wearing sneakers than it is along an
icy sidewalk wearing leather-soled shoes. So you
know that the force of friction depends on the
kinds of surfaces that are rubbing against each
other. To find out which kinds of surfaces provide
more or less friction, you can use an experiment
like the one shown in Figure 6.

If you don't have blocks, **ask an adult to cut
them** from a length of 2-in × 4-in lumber. Then
you can use sandpaper to smooth and round the
edges of one large surface and one narrow surface

on one or more of the blocks. Place one of the blocks, smooth side down, on the board. (A Masonite board is excellent but any smooth board will do.) Then slowly lift the board, tapping it with your finger so that any localized "stickiness" doesn't prevent the block from sliding. Use a ruler or yardstick to measure the height of the end of the board when the block slides.

The height can serve as a measure of the frictional force. To see that this is true, place a heavy toy truck on the board. Attach a spring scale or long, thin rubber band to the truck. As you raise the end of the board (Figure 7), you'll see that the force needed to keep the truck from rolling down the hill increases. So if you have to raise the board higher to make the block slide, there must be more friction keeping the block in place. As you can see, the steeper the board, the greater the force. It's the same thing that you find on your bicycle. The steeper the hill, the more your bike speeds up because the force gets bigger as the hill gets steeper.

Now try some different surfaces on the blocks. Two wide rubber bands can be used to give the block a rubber surface as shown in Figure 8. Thumbtacks can be inserted on the unsanded side of the block to make a metal surface. Felt pads can be stuck on to make a felt surface. You can tape sandpaper, aluminum foil, waxed paper, construction paper, and other surfaces of your own design to the block. Which surface has the most friction? Which has the least?

You can also change the *surface* of the board by covering it with various types of paper or foil

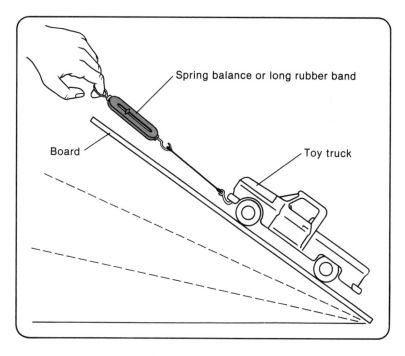

Figure 7. What happens to the force
as the "hill" gets steeper?

or by using boards of the same length made of
different materials. Which combination of board
and block surfaces has the most friction? The least
friction? Why must boards made of different materials have the same length if you are to compare
the frictional forces?

Does the area of the surface affect the friction?
To find out, turn the block onto its narrow sanded
side. How does the height you have to raise the
board to make the block slide now compare with
the height you had to use before? How does the

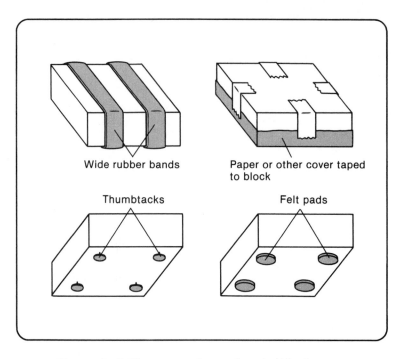

Figure 8. Different surfaces for the blocks may change the friction between block and board.

friction on the narrow side compare with the friction on the wide side?

Suppose you double the weight of the block by placing an identical block on top of the first one. Do you think the friction will increase? If you think it will, does this mean you'll have to raise the board higher? This is a little tricky. If doubling the weight doubles the friction, the double block will slide at the *same height* as the single block. To see why, hang the toy truck from a spring scale or a long, thin rubber band. Measure the weight of

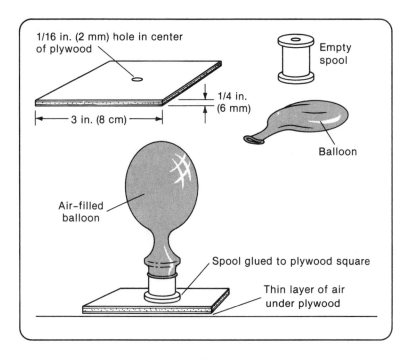

Figure 9. Building a "frictionless" air-car

the truck with the spring scale or as the length of the stretched rubber band. Now find some object or objects that have the same weight as the truck. Then place the truck on the board. Tip the board to a convenient angle and measure the force needed to keep the truck from rolling. Without changing the angle of the board, add the object or objects to the truck so as to double its weight. You'll find that it now takes just twice as much force to keep the truck from rolling.

Do you think a stack of three blocks will triple the friction? How can you find out if you are right?

You can't get rid of friction entirely. But you can come close by building the small air-car shown in Figure 9. **Ask an adult to help you cut the small plywood square and drill the small hole in the center.** Then you can sandpaper the surface of the wood and glue the wooden spool to the plywood square. Once the glue is dry, you can attach the balloon and try sliding your air-car along a smooth table top or Formica covered surface. How can you tell that the air-car is almost frictionless? How can you use the air-car to find out whether a surface is level or not?

ROLLING WHEELS AND SLIDING WHEELS

Friction has many practical applications. Just try walking without it some icy morning. Many practical devices have been made to reduce friction. None is more important than the wheel or roller, which was one of man's earliest and cleverest inventions. In this experiment, you'll see just how much friction is eliminated by the wheel. You'll also see how front and rear wheel brakes are designed to reduce the chances of a car going into a spin on slippery hills.

Things You'll Need

- rigid box—wood or hard plastic
- concrete block or other heavy object
- spring scale (optional)
- rollers—wood or metal dowels
- toy car or truck with free-turning wheels
- long, wide board
- ruler
- rubber bands

Place a rigid box on a smooth, level sidewalk, basement floor, or driveway. Feel, or measure with a spring scale, how hard you have to pull to make the box slide along at a constant slow speed. Place a concrete block or some other heavy object in the box. Again, feel or measure how hard it is to move the box now. Does friction increase with weight?

Now place the box and the weight on some rollers. Place a few more rollers in front of the box so you'll be able to move the box over a short distance. See Figure 10. How hard is it to move the box now? How much have the rollers (wheels) reduced friction?

As you've seen, rolling wheels reduce friction. Now take a look at sliding wheels. Take the toy car, and place it on the wide board. How high do you have to lift the end of the board before the car will roll? Now apply "brakes" to the wheels by using rubber bands as shown in Figure 11. How high do

Figure 10. A heavy box on "wheels"

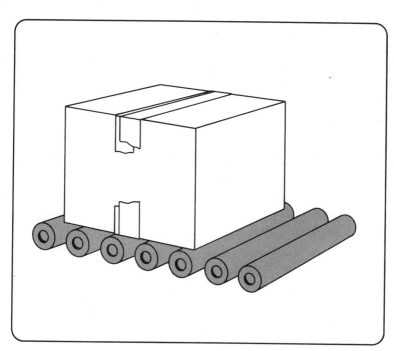

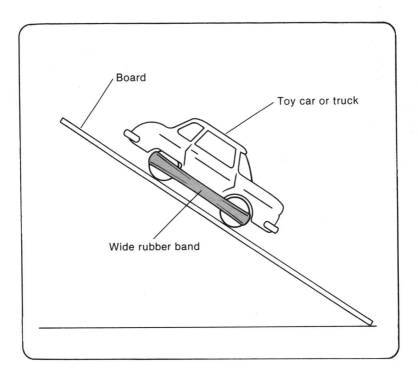

Figure 11. A toy car with its "brakes" on.
The wide rubber band "brake" prevents
the wheels from turning.

you have to lift the board to make the car slide
now? Repeat the experiment with brakes on *only*
the front wheels or *only* the rear wheels. Does it
make any difference whether it is the front or rear
wheels that are braked? What is the difference?

Based on what you've seen, when a driver
steps on the brake pedal of a car, which brakes do
you think grab first, the front brakes or the rear?
What makes you think so?

STRAW TOWERS

David Webster, with whom I wrote several books, was responsible for this experiment, which is another of my favorites. A similar experiment can be found in his book *Towers*. It involves building towers from soda straws. In addition to being fun and a possible source of competition, it also teaches some basic principles about construction.

Things You'll Need

- soda straws
- common pins
- clay
- sheet of cardboard

Look carefully at a soda straw. It is a tower in itself. If you stand the straw on one end and push straight down on the other end, you'll find the straw is very strong. If you use the straw to make a bridge between two books, you'll find that it is easily bent in the middle. A straw is very strong lengthwise, but not very strong sidewise.

If you have a paper soda straw, make four creases along its length so that it becomes a square straw instead of a round one. Is the square straw as strong as the round one was? Does the shape of a straw affect its strength?

To make a really tall tower from straws you'll need to join the straws by sliding them together or connecting them with pins as shown in Figure 12.

How tall a tower can you build from soda straws by connecting them in either of these two ways? You can use a piece of clay to support the bottommost straw. What happens if you wave a cardboard sheet up and down to produce a wind that blows against your tower?

To make a tower that can withstand strong

winds, you'll need a broader base. You could stack straws side by side, but that would take a lot of straws. A more practical way that is used in building many real towers is to build a framework.

Before you begin building, make a square frame like the one shown in Figure 13a. Notice how wobbly this structure is. To give it more strength you need only add a diagonal straw to make the square into two triangles (Figure 13b). Notice how much firmer the triangles are than the square.

Figure 12. Two ways to fasten soda straws together

Figure 13. (facing page) A triangular structure
is much stronger than a square one.

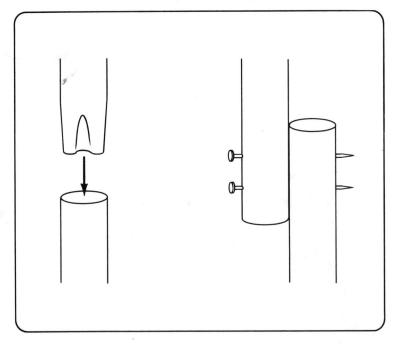

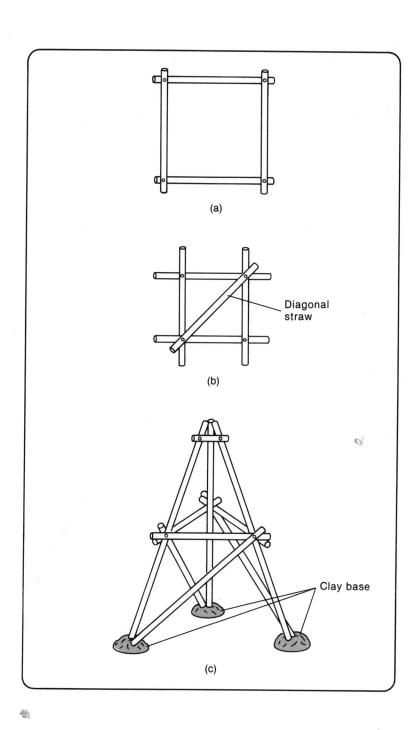

(a)

Diagonal
straw

(b)

Clay base

(c)

With a knowledge of diagonals in mind, see how high you can build a straw tower that is "wind resistant." One simple model in its beginning stages is shown in Figure 13c. You might invite your friends in and have a contest to see who can build the tallest wind-resistant tower from a box of straws and common pins. A week later you might have another contest: who can build the tallest tower from a pound of modeling clay? Or who can build the strongest bridge from a box of soda straws?

FALLING AND FLYING

Many people find it hard to believe that heavy objects and light objects will fall side by side, but it's true, as this experiment will show. In a vacuum it's perfectly true. In air, however, there is always a frictional force between the air and the object. It's called air resistance. Like all friction, air resistance pushes against the object in motion. As a result, objects moving through air do not move as fast as they would in a vacuum.

It's also true that for nearly a hundred years humans have been able to travel through air in any direction they wish without falling. We've found a way to make the air provide a lifting force when the wings of an airplane move through it.

Things You'll Need

- two balls: one light, one heavy
- several sheets of paper
- a book
- scissors
- handkerchief or linen cloth
- 4 strings about 10 in (25 cm) long
- two steel washers

Hold a heavy ball, such as a baseball, in one hand, and a lighter ball, such as a golf ball, in the other. Hold the two balls with your arms extended out from your body. Release them at the same

46

time. You'll find that they fall side by side and strike the floor at the same moment. (Or very nearly so. It's not easy to release them at exactly the same moment.)

You might even like to try this experiment from a greater height. **Ask an adult to release the two balls from a second-story window** while you watch from below. Again, you'll see that they fall side by side.

Repeat the experiment, but this time replace one of the balls with a sheet of paper. Do the ball and the paper fall at the same rate? As you can see, air resistance slows down the paper much more than the ball. Now squeeze the paper into a small ball. Again, drop it at the same time as one of the balls. How do their rates of fall compare this time?

Here's another way to reduce air resistance. Drop a hardcover book and a sheet of paper from the same height. Drop the book so it will land flat, on its wide hard cover, not on its binding.

You probably weren't surprised to see the book reach the floor first. Now place the paper on the book as shown in Figure 14. If the paper is bigger than the book, use scissors to trim it until it is a bit smaller than the book's cover. Now release the book with the paper resting on its front cover. Why do they fall together?

When a skydiver jumps from an airplane, he or she falls with increasing speed for a while. But air resistance increases with speed, and soon the skydiver reaches what's called a terminal speed. After reaching terminal speed, his or her speed downward remains constant at about 120 mph (190 kph) or about 175 ft/s (54 m/s). Skydivers

47

A time-lapse photo of two falling balls. How can you tell that they are accelerating? On which ball is the air resistance greater?

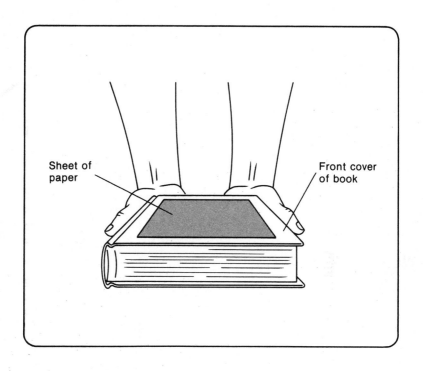

Figure 14. Will the sheet of paper and book fall together, or will the book fall faster?

can change their terminal speeds by changing the air resistance. As you know, a crumpled piece of paper falls faster than one that's spread out. Similarly, a skydiver in spread-eagle style will fall slower than one curled up like a cannon ball. At some point, the skydiver opens a parachute, which has a large surface area. After the parachute opens, the skydiver descends at a much slower speed, one slow enough to ensure a safe collision with the ground.

Make a small model parachute from a handkerchief or a piece of linen cloth and four strings

(Above) These skydivers increase the air resistance that slows them down by spreading out their arms and legs.

Figure 15. (facing page) Some designs for long-flying paper airplanes

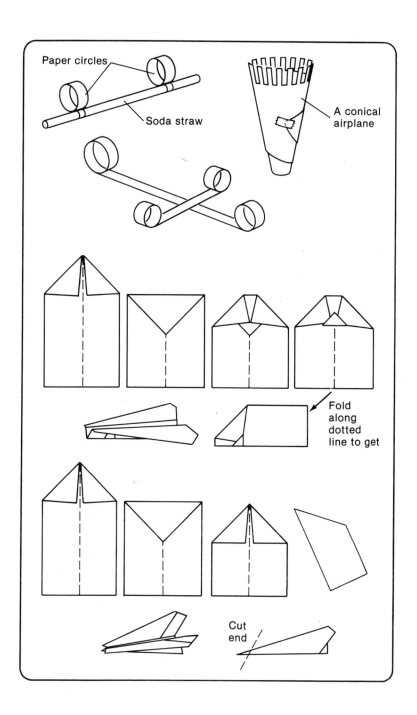

Paper circles

Soda straw

A conical airplane

Fold along dotted line to get

Cut end

about 10 in (25 cm) long. Tie one end of each string to a corner of the handkerchief and the other to a pair of washers that represent a skydiver. Close your fist around the "parachute and skydiver" and throw them into the air. Why does the parachute descend so much more slowly than it ascended?

It's also possible to build machines that will not fall—machines that will ascend into the air and travel great distances before descending safely back to Earth. You know such machines as airplanes. They're very expensive, but you might like to build a model airplane. A simple one with a rubber-band motor can be purchased at most toy stores or hobby shops. If not, you can at least make a paper airplane. They do come down, but they can be made to travel amazing distances in a large room. Some designs for paper airplanes are shown in Figure 15. You might like to make some of your own design. You might also like to invite your friends to a paper airplane contest, and see who can design the airplane that will fly the farthest or stay airborne the longest.

3

EXPERIMENTS WITH BIOLOGY

Biology is the study of life—a rather broad subject. It includes all plants and animals. My own favorite biology experiments involve the way we humans use our senses and how our senses are often fooled. Some of those experiments are in this chapter. I've also included experiments with plants and animals other than humans.

WHICH IS LONGER, HORIZONTAL OR VERTICAL?

You may think the title of this experiment is either wrong or a mistake. But actually it's a good question in terms of the way we see things. In terms of measurement, a mile is a mile whether we're measuring the distance to the horizon or to a cloud vertically above us. But, as you will soon discover, your brain does not interpret distance in the same way vertically that it does horizontally.

Things You'll Need

- blackboard and chalk, or large sheet of white paper and marking pen,
- straightedge, such as a yardstick or meter stick
- tape and paste or glue
- scissors
- pieces of black, white, and gray construction paper
- paper towels

Use a straightedge to draw a horizontal line about 18 in (45 cm) long. Draw the line on a blackboard or on a large sheet of white paper taped to a wall. Ask someone to draw freehand a vertical line up from the center of the horizontal line. He or she should draw it equal in length to the horizontal line. Then use a yardstick or a meter stick to measure the two lines.

Repeat this experiment a number of times with different people. Which line is almost always longer?

Do you see now why a tree looks much longer when it is standing than it does after it has been cut down? Or why those clouds that look to be skimming the treetops are really much higher?

Here's another experiment that will make you wonder if you can really believe what you see. With scissors, cut a circle from a sheet of gray construction paper. Tape a piece of white and a piece of black construction paper together. Then paste the gray circle onto the sheets of black and white construction paper as shown in Figure 16. Lay a yardstick, meter stick, or some other straightedge vertically across the diameter of the circle. How does the color of the gray circle on the white side compare with the color of the gray circle on the black side?

Now for a real mystery! Slowly move the stick used to divide the circle to the right or left. Notice how it "drags" the gray color with it. Can you drag the gray in the other direction? You can really amaze your friends with this experiment.

Now look at Figure 17. You see a white square, but look carefully. There is no white square. There are only notches in four sets of concentric circles.

54

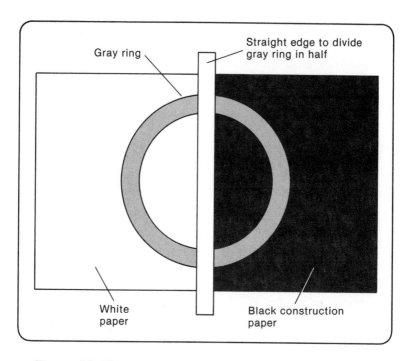

Figure 16. The strange appearance of a gray ring on a sheet of paper that is divided into black and white halves

Figure 17. The little white square that isn't there

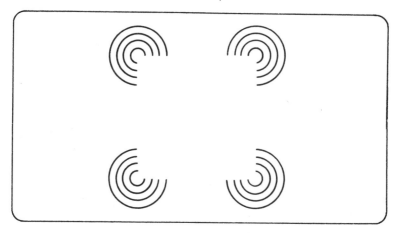

EFFECTS OF DARKNESS ON BALANCE AND HEARING

This experiment will help you to answer these questions: Do light and sound play a role in your ability to maintain your balance? Does darkness affect your ability to hear? At first, these questions may seem silly. What could light and sound possibly have to do with balance, and how could darkness affect our hearing? But blind people frequently hear things that people with sight do not. These experiments will help you to see that seemingly unrelated factors may actually be related in ways you might not anticipate.

Things You'll Need

- short length of 2-in × 4-in lumber
- large open space— room or lawn
- watch or clock with second hand
- friend to help you
- room that can be made totally dark (or a good blindfold)
- meter stick or yardstick
- good blindfold

Place a short length of a piece of 2-in × 4-in lumber on a flat floor or a level lawn. **To avoid getting hurt, be sure that there are no objects nearby that you might fall on.** It's best to do this in the center of a large room or lawn. With your eyes open, have a friend with a watch or a clock with a second hand measure the time that you can balance yourself while standing on one foot on the board. Repeat the experiment standing on the other foot. Then you can test your friend to see how long he or she can stand on one foot.

Now repeat the experiment, but this time place your foot on the board and then close your eyes before you stand on one foot. Repeat the experiment standing on the other foot with your eyes closed. How does the time that you can balance with your eyes closed compare with the time you can balance with your eyes open?

Why are you less able to maintain your balance with your eyes closed? Is it because your eyes are closed, or is it because it's dark when you close your eyes? To find out, try the experiment at night in a dark room. Are you able to keep your balance better with your eyes open even if you can't see? If you can't make the room totally dark, use a blindfold. Use a good one, one that allows you to open your eyes but admits no light.

To see if darkness affects hearing, have a friend hold a ticking watch or small clock near your ear as you sit in a chair. Then have him or her move the watch or clock farther and farther from your ear keeping it at the same height. Tell your friend at what point you can no longer hear the ticking. How far away was the sound when you could no longer hear it?

Repeat the experiment with your eyes closed. How far away was the sound this time when you could no longer hear it?

Repeat it again while wearing a good blindfold. Be sure the blindfold does not cover your ear. Do it first with your eyes open under the blindfold and then with your eyes closed.

Here are some questions to ask yourself:

- Can you hear better in darkness than in light?
- Does it matter whether your eyes are closed or open?
- Does it matter which ear you use?
  Try the experiment with other people. Are the results the same?

MAKING SEEDS GROW

If you have a garden, you probably read the directions on the package to decide how deep to plant the seeds. What do you think will happen if you plant the seeds deeper or shallower than the depth recommended? In this experiment you'll find out what happens when you plant seeds at different depths. Then you'll test some other factors to see how they affect the seeds' development.

This experiment will help you to become a good observer. It will also help you to see why scientists are so concerned about measuring things. Without a ruler to measure the seeds you might not be aware of some of the changes that are taking place.

Things You'll Need

- large (1 in) stones or marbles
- aquarium or tall, wide-mouth jars
- sand or gravel
- potting soil
- corn seeds
- black paper or cardboard
- tape or rubber bands
- water (If your tap water is chlorinated, let it stand for several days before adding to soil.)
- notebook
- ruler
- thermometer
- loam, sand, gravel, and clay

Place about a 1-inch-deep (3 cm) layer of the large stones or marbles on the bottom of the aquarium or wide-mouth jars. Then add about the same depth of sand or gravel. These lower layers of soil will allow the water to drain past the seeds and prevent them from rotting. Then add about 8 inches (20 cm) of potting soil. The aquarium or jars should be kept in a warm room.

Place four or five corn seeds on the surface of the soil. Cover another four or five corn seeds with about an inch (3 cm) of the potting soil. Plant a third group of seeds about 2 inches (5 cm) deep, a fourth group 4 inches (10 cm) deep, and so on, until you reach a depth where the seeds are very

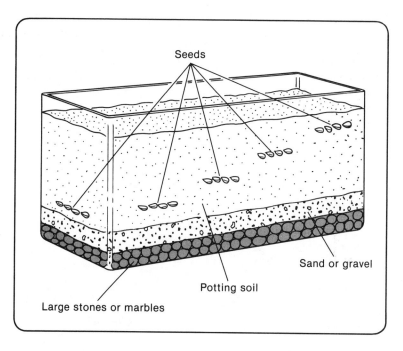

Seeds

Sand or gravel

Potting soil

Large stones or marbles

Figure 18. How does the depth of seeds in the ground affect their germination and growth?

near the gravel. (See Figure 18.) Be sure to plant the seeds next to the glass so you can look at them every day. When you are not looking at the seeds, keep the sides of the aquarium or jars covered with black paper or cardboard. That way the seeds will be in darkness, just as they would be in a garden. The paper can be held in place with tape or rubber bands.

Add water to the soil occasionally to keep it moist but not wet. Each day, record in your notebook all the things you observe about the seeds at each depth. For the first day or two you might not observe anything. But if you use a ruler to measure the seeds, you may find that they are getting larger. Later, you may notice that roots and stems begin to grow out of the seed. This is called *germination*. Use your ruler to measure the lengths of the roots and stems every day.

Which way do the roots and stems grow? What happens if the seeds are "upside down"? Does the depth of the seeds affect the time it takes them to germinate? Does it affect the rate at which the roots and stems grow?

After about six weeks, for each group of seeds planted at a different depth, cut off the parts of the plants that are above the soil. Keep each set of plants separate and use a balance scale to weigh each set. Which plants weigh the most? What seems to be the best depth to plant corn seeds?

To see how temperature affects the germination of different seeds, you'll need three wide-mouth glass or plastic jars. Nearly fill each jar with stones or marbles, sand or gravel, and potting soil, as before. Plant four corn seeds on one side of each jar. On the opposite side of each jar, plant four pea seeds as shown in Figure 19. Cover the sides of the jars with black paper or cardboard as before. Place one jar in a cold place such as a refrigerator. Place another in a very warm place. The top of the refrigerator near the back might be such a place. When the refrigerator is running, you can feel warm air rising from around the coils in the back. The third jar should be placed in a cool place, such as near a basement wall.

You can use a thermometer to measure the temperature near each jar. Be sure the temperature in each of the three places stays reasonably con-

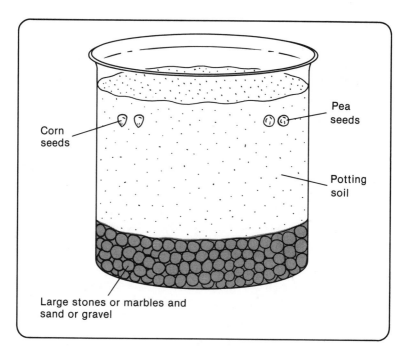

Figure 19. How does temperature affect
the growth of corn and pea seeds?

stant and differs significantly from the other loca-
tions. Temperatures of 40° F (5° C), 55° F (12° C),
and 75° F (25° C) are good. Throughout the experiment add water to keep the soil moist but not
wet. You'll probably need to add more water to the
warm jar than the cold one because more water
will evaporate from the warm soil.

How does temperature affect the germination
of the seeds? How does it affect the growth of the
plants after germination? Which seeds and plants
seem to do better in cooler temperatures? In
warmer temperatures?

Do you think plants will grow better in one type of soil than in another? For example, will seedlings grow better in loam, sand, gravel, clay, or some combination? Design an experiment of your own to find out.

Is soil necessary for seeds to germinate? You may be surprised to find that seeds will germinate without soil. Just put some corn, radish, or bean seeds on damp paper towels in a closed container. Keep the towels damp and you'll soon see the seeds begin to germinate. Will seeds germinate faster if they are soaked overnight before being placed on damp towels or in soil?

You can buy birdseed at a supermarket. People buy these seeds to feed to birds that live near their homes. Using what you have learned about the conditions necessary for seeds to germinate, design an experiment to find out if the seeds sold as birdseed will germinate.

GRASS IN THE DARK

You may have heard that the green color of leaves and grass is due to chlorophyll, the substance that gives plants their green color. You may have heard too that it is chlorophyll that makes it possible for plants to manufacture their own food. Plants can combine carbon dioxide and water, in the presence of chlorophyll, to produce food in the form of sugar or starch. The energy needed for this process comes from sunlight. The experiments required to show how plants do this are very complicated. But here's an experiment you can do that will show you what happens when grass is kept in darkness.

Things You'll Need

- grassy area
- short, wide board

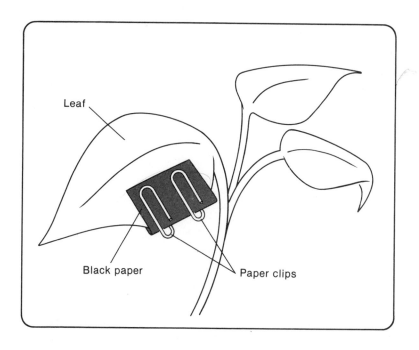

Figure 20. What happens to the part of
a leaf that's kept in darkness?

Find a grassy place in your yard or at a park or
playground where your experiment will not be
disturbed. *Ask permission before you begin the
experiment.* You can keep a small grassy patch in
darkness by placing a short, wide board on the
grass.

Every day or two look under the board to see
what's happening to the grass. Does its color
change? After there seem to be no further
changes, remove the board. Every day or two go
back and look at the same patch of grass. What
happens to the grass?

Does light seem to be necessary for grass to make chlorophyll? If grass loses its chlorophyll, can it ever make chlorophyll again?

See if you can predict what will happen if you cover a part of a geranium leaf with black construction paper. Hold the paper in place with paper clips as shown in Figure 20. Look under the paper every day or two to see what's happening to the leaf. When there are no further changes, remove the black paper and continue to check the leaf every day or two. Does the leaf respond to light in the same way that the grass did?

GROWING PLANTS ON A TURNTABLE

If you did the experiments with seeds in "Making Seeds Grow," you know that no matter how you plant the seeds, roots grow downward and stems grow upward. Stems resist the pull of gravity. In fact, they grow in a direction that is opposite to the direction that gravity pulls them.

You know that when you ride on a merry-go-round or a playground whirligig, it feels as if there is a force pushing you outward. This force is called a centrifugal force. It appears whenever you ride on something that moves in a circle. If plants were grown on a merry-go-round, how would they respond? Would their stems continue to grow straight upward opposite to the pull of gravity? Or would they grow upward *and inward* in response to the centrifugal force as well as the force of gravity?

This is an interesting question. And it's one that can be easily answered by experiment. All you need do is germinate some seeds on a spinning platform.

Things You'll Need

- old turntable (record player)
- thick cardboard (Cut into round shape with scissors or **have an adult cut the cardboard with a sharp knife**)
- deep pie pan
- potting soil
- twenty corn seeds

Cover the surface of the old turntable with the thick, round piece of cardboard as shown in Figure 21. Fill the deep pie pan with moist potting soil. Then push about twenty corn seeds an inch (3 cm) or so beneath the soil at various places in the pan. Cover the seeds with the soil and place the pan on the turntable.

Set the turntable spinning in a well-lighted room. Keep the soil moist but not wet by adding water occasionally. As the seeds germinate and grow out of the soil, which way do they grow? Do they grow straight upward, or do they grow upward and inward? Do the plants near the center of the turntable grow in the same direction as those near the edge of turntable?

Based on your observations, is the centrifugal force greater near the center or the edge of the turntable? What makes you think so?

HUNTING INSECTS	Things You'll Need
This experiment should convince you that insects are the most common animal on Earth. I am always amazed at the number and variety of insects that can be captured in this very simple experiment.	• insect net (or cheesecloth bag, wire coat hanger, string, old broom handle, and tape) • large transparent plastic bag • an old bed sheet

If you don't have an insect net you can use for this experiment, you can make one from a cheesecloth bag, a wire coat hanger, string, an old broom handle, and some tape.

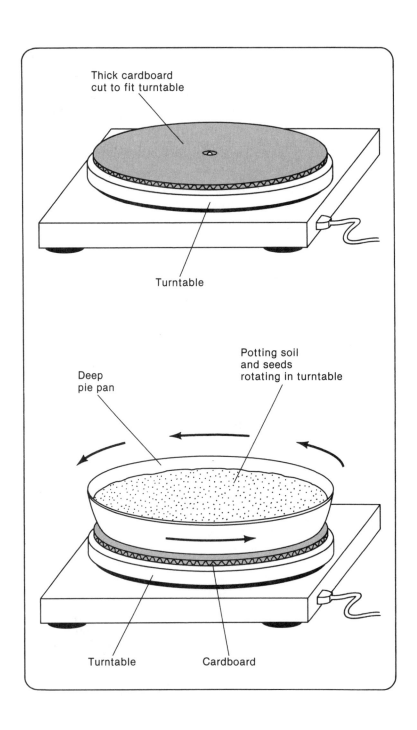

Thick cardboard
cut to fit turntable

Turntable

Potting soil
and seeds
rotating in turntable

Deep
pie pan

Turntable   Cardboard

To collect insects just walk through an open field where tall grass and/or weeds are growing. Swing the net back and forth in front of you as you walk. After you've swept a swath across the field, twist the bag around several times at its center to trap the insects. Place the net inside a large clear plastic bag. Tie the neck of the bag to the handle of the net. Then untwist the net and turn it inside out within the plastic bag.

How many insects did you catch? How many kinds of insects can you see? Can you identify them?

Repeat this experiment at different times of the year. When are insects most abundant? Are the kinds of insects that you capture in May different from those you capture in August or September? Would there be a season when you'd expect to find no insects?

Here's another way to capture insects. Place an old sheet underneath a bush. Then shake the bush. How many insects fall onto the sheet. How many kinds of insects do you find? Are they the same kinds you found in the field?

Figure 21. Have you ever felt centrifugal force when riding a playground whirligig? Will the plants instinctively defy physical forces (in this case by growing upwards *and* inwards)? Which way will seedlings grow on a rotating turntable?

Buy about a gross (twelve dozen) of mealworms from a pet store or a biological supply house. Keep them in a plastic or glass container that is at least 6 inches (15 cm) across. The bottom of the container should be covered with a layer of food about 2 inches (5 cm) deep. They will eat oatmeal, wheat bran, or chicken laying mash. The food should be kept dry to prevent molds from growing. The animals can get water from carrots, potatoes, or apples placed, uncut, on the dry food. The entire container should be covered with a sheet of heavy cardboard to reduce drying and to contain the mealworms.

When the fruit or vegetable appears to be dried out, replace it with a fresh sample. If you see mold developing, or if you notice the odor of ammonia, remove the animals and place them in another container with fresh food.

While you are waiting for the mealworm larvae to develop into pupae, you can use some of them for the experiments described below. Once the larvae begin changing into pupae, remove the pupae and put them in another container with a small amount of food. When adult beetles emerge from the pupae, transfer the adults back to the original mealworm culture. The pupae should be isolated to prevent them from being eaten by the larvae or by the adult beetles. After the adults are returned to the original container, watch for small eggs that hatch into the tiny mealworm larvae.

The behavior of mealworm larvae can be studied by experiment. Place several mealworms on a sheet of paper. Fold a sheet of heavy black construction paper and place it over half the paper as shown in Figure 22. The mealworms now have a choice. They can remain on the paper in the light or go under the black paper into the dark. Watch them for a few minutes. Do they seem to prefer light or darkness?

Place a mealworm on a table- or countertop. Touch the animal gently with the head of a toothpick or a pin. How does it respond? Does its response depend on where you touch it?

Dip a cotton swab into some vinegar. Slowly bring the swab near (but not touching) a mealworm's head. How does the animal respond? Is its response different if you hold the swab near its tail or its side? Use another swab to see how the mealworm responds to ammonia.

Hold a flashlight near a mealworm's head.

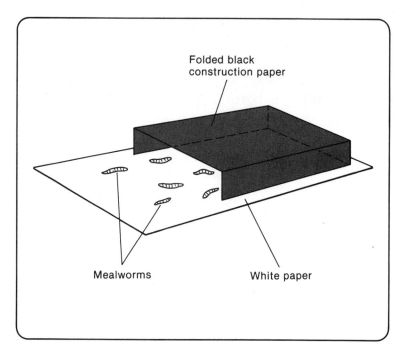

Figure 22. Do mealworms prefer light or darkness?

Does it respond to the bright light? Does it respond any differently if you hold the flashlight near its back end?

To see how a mealworm responds to high temperature, **ask an adult** to bring a hot soldering iron near (*but not touching*) the mealworm. Why is a soldering iron better than a burning match for this experiment?

Will a mealworm respond to sound? How does a mealworm respond to cold temperatures? Design experiments to answer these questions.

4

EXPERIMENTS WITH LIGHT AND ASTRONOMY

Anyone who looks up at the stars cannot help but feel dwarfed by the vastness of space.

Consider the following:

• It takes the light leaving the nearest star, which is our sun, about 8.6 minutes (516 seconds) to reach us. We know this because the sun is about 96,000,000 miles away and light travels at a speed of 186,000 miles per second.

• Light from the next nearest star (Alpha Centauri) requires 4.3 years to reach Earth. Knowing the speed of light and the fact that there are 31,536,000 seconds in a year, you can figure out how far away that star is. You'll find it's close to 25 trillion miles—a billion times the earth's circumference.

In this chapter you'll explore not only the sun, moon, and stars but some of the properties of light that enable us to see and magnify these celestial bodies. You'll learn how light reflects and how it bends when it passes from one transparent material to another.

A FUNDAMENTAL LAW OF REFLECTION

The first scientific principle I became aware of might be called the "peekaboo" law of light. I was playing peekaboo with my mother using a mirror when I realized that if she could see me in the mirror, I could see her and vice versa. Years later I could recite that the path followed by light rays is reversible, but I knew it at the gut level long before I studied physics in high school. In this experiment, you'll play mirror peekaboo and then see how the peekaboo law works.

Things You'll Need

- large mirror on wall
- two small mirrors and lump of clay
- one-slit mask made by cutting a narrow slit in a folded piece of black construction paper
- lamp
- scissors
- white paper
- protractor

Check up on the peekaboo law for yourself. Stand with a friend in front of a mirror. Can you see the image of your friend's eyes in the mirror? Can he or she see the image of your eyes? Now move to one side of the mirror so that you cannot see your own image. Can you see your friend's image? Can he or she see your image? Have both you and your friend move to different places on opposite sides of the mirror. If you can see your friend's eyes in the mirror, can he or she see your eyes? Can you find any set of positions where you can see the image of your friend's eyes in the mirror but he or she can't see the image of your eyes?

(Facing page) A mirror with a curved surface can create funny images. Amusement park mirrors can be convex, concave or cylindrical. The concave mirror surface in this photo magnifies the boy's head.

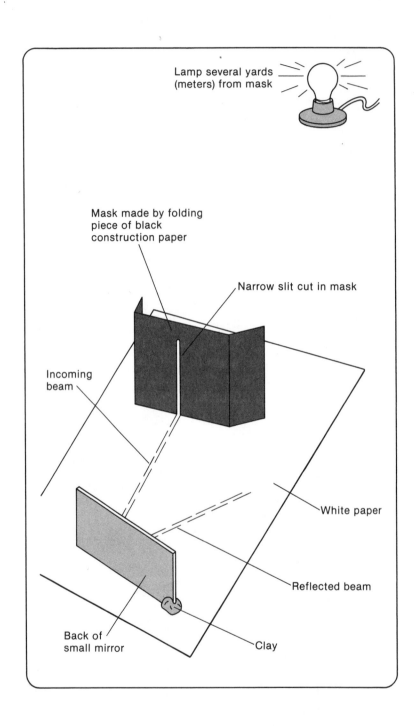

Lamp several yards (meters) from mask

Mask made by folding piece of black construction paper

Narrow slit cut in mask

Incoming beam

White paper

Reflected beam

Back of small mirror

Clay

To see why your friend can always see the image of your eyes when you can see his or her image, set up the mirror, one-slit mask, and lamp in a *dark room* as shown in Figure 23. The mirror can be supported by a small piece of clay. Make the slit in the black construction paper about $1/16$ inch (1 mm) wide. Scissors can be used to cut the paper. The light coming through the slit should make a sharp, narrow beam. Use a pencil to draw a line along the front edge of the mirror resting on a sheet of white paper. Then draw lines along the center of the light beam before and after it strikes the mirror. How does the angle between the mirror and the incoming beam (see Figure 24a) compare with the angle between the mirror and the reflected beam? The angles can be measured with a protractor.

Turn the mirror so that the incoming beam hits the mirror at different angles. In each case measure the angles between the mirror and the two beams. How does the angle between the incoming beam and the mirror compare with the angle between the reflected beam and the mirror?

Now use a second mirror to reflect the reflected beam back along its path to the first mirror as shown in Figure 24b. Notice that it follows the same path, but in the opposite direction. Will this still be true if the first mirror is set at a different angle? Do you see now why the peekaboo law works?

Figure 23. Making and reflecting a narrow beam of light

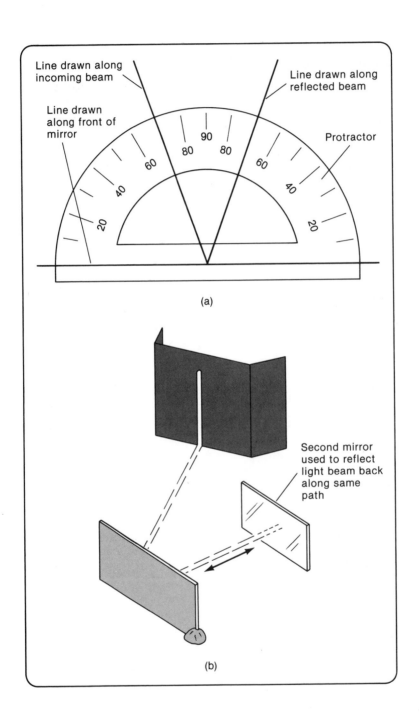

Line drawn along incoming beam

Line drawn along reflected beam

Line drawn along front of mirror

Protractor

90

80 80

60 60

40 40

20 20

(a)

Second mirror used to reflect light beam back along same path

(b)

BENDING LIGHT, AND THE REAPPEARING COIN

Light bends sharply when it passes from one transparent substance to another, such as from air to water or from glass to air. This bending is a fundamental property of light. It explains why a swimming pool looks shallower than it really is, or why we see inverted or enlarged images with a hand lens. It also explains why the coin you'll see disappear in a cup can be made to reappear by pouring water into the cup. The coin reappears because light bends when it passes from one transparent material to another. It's this same property of light that allows us to use lenses to make images that we can see on a screen. You've seen such images at a movie or on a screen in front of a slide projector.

Things You'll Need

- two drinking glasses
- water
- long pencil
- two identical coins
- teacup
- small pitcher
- hand lens (magnifying glass)
- eyedropper

To see that light bends when it passes from water to air, simply put a pencil in a glass of water and look at it from the side. Notice how the pencil appears to be "broken" at the water line. The light coming through the water and glass to the air is bent and reaches your eye from a different angle than the light that comes directly to your eye through air. What else is different about the pencil as a result of light coming through water before it enters the air?

Figure 24. A) Comparing the angles that an incoming and a reflected beam make with a mirror. B) Reflecting light back along the same path

77

Place identical coins on the bottom of each of two identical drinking glasses. Put the glasses side by side, and fill one glass with water. Now look down through the two glasses. You'll notice that the coin in the water-filled glass looks bigger and closer. The diagram in Figure 25 shows how the bending of light as it passes from the water-

Figure 25. A) Light beams travel from the coin through air in straight lines. The coin is seen to be at points where rays come from. B) Light bends as it passes from water to air. The dotted lines show the extensions of the bent light beams (rays) that come into the air from the water. The coin appears to be where the dotted lines meet. That's where the rays *appear* to come from.

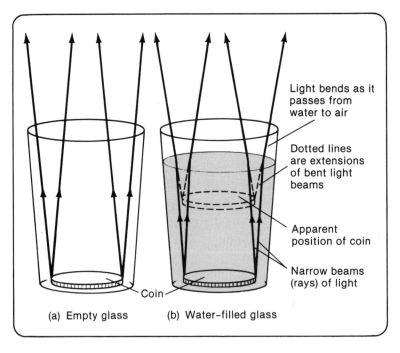

Light bends as it passes from water to air

Dotted lines are extensions of bent light beams

Apparent position of coin

Narrow beams (rays) of light

Coin

(a) Empty glass   (b) Water-filled glass

filled glass to the air makes the coin appear to be closer. Because it appears to be closer, it also appears to be larger.

Now place one of the coins on the bottom of a teacup. Lower your head until the coin, hidden by the side of the cup, just disappears from your sight. While you hold your head in this position, ask someone to slowly pour water into the cup from a small pitcher. The coin will mysteriously reappear. Use what you know about the bending of light to explain why it reappears.

Finally, you can use a hand lens to make images on a screen. At night, turn on a single lamp in an otherwise dark room. Hold a hand lens close to a light-colored wall across the room from the lamp. Move the lens toward and away from the wall until you see a clear image of the lamp on the wall. Is the image right side up or upside down?

The light coming from the lamp is brought together to form an image. Figure 26 shows how this is done for light rays coming from one point on an object. Light coming from every other point on the object is brought together in the same way to form an entire image. Can you use the hand lens to make images of other objects that emit light? **Don't use the lens to look at the sun. In fact, never look directly at the sun. It can seriously damage your eyes.**

Hold the lens close to some print in this book. What do you notice about the size of the print as you look through the lens? What happens to the image you see through the lens as you move the lens farther from the print?

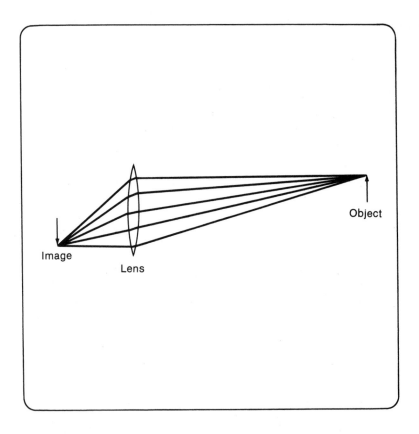

Figure 26. Light from a distant object is bent by a lens to form an image of the object. The lens in your eye forms images on the retina at the back of your eye.

Because of its shape, a drop of water will act like a lens. Use an eyedropper to carefully place a drop of water on some fine print on a *glossy* page in a magazine. Compare the size of the print under the drop with print that lies outside the water. What evidence do you have that water, like glass or plastic, can serve as a lens?

UP PERISCOPE!

Now that you know how light reflects and bends you might like to make a periscope. You probably know that submarines have periscopes. By sticking a periscope above the ocean's surface, submariners can see what's going on above the water without having to surface.

In this experiment you'll see that periscopes can be made from mirrors or from prisms. You won't use your periscope in a submarine, but you can use it to see around corners. The periscope is one example of how the reflection and refraction of light are used to make a practical device. Of course, there are many more. They range from simple hand mirrors to cameras, microscopes, telescopes, and lasers.

Things You'll Need

- two small mirrors and clay
- one-slit mask made by cutting a narrow slit in a folded piece of black construction paper
- lamp
- scissors
- white paper
- two 45-45-90 prisms

To see how periscopes work, take two mirrors and use them to reflect a narrow beam of light as shown in Figure 27. Notice that if you turn the mirror so that it makes an angle of 45 degrees with the light beam, the direction of the beam will be diverted by 90 degrees. By doing this twice, you can divert the beam along a second path that is parallel to the first one.

If you place a 45-45-90 prism on the beam, you'll see that it will bend the light when the light hits the surface at an angle. In fact, if you turn it just right, you can break the beam of white light into a rainbow of colors that emerge from the other side of the prism. But see what happens when the light hits the longest surface head-on as shown in Figure 28a. In this case, the light doesn't bend. Instead it goes straight through and

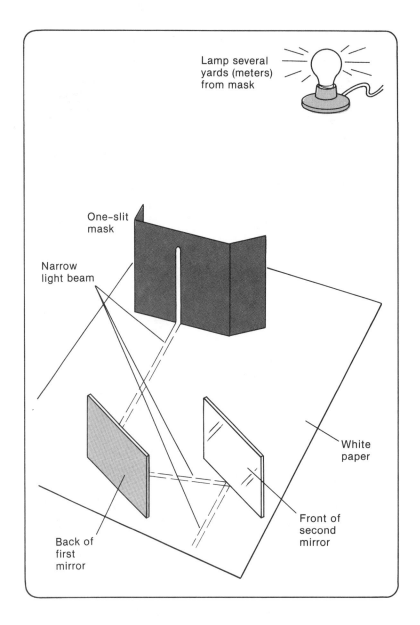

Figure 27. A model of a periscope
made from two mirrors

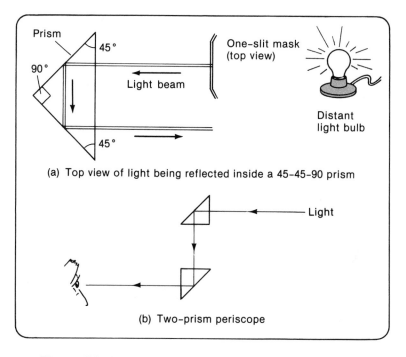

Figure 28. A) Top view of light being reflected inside
a 45-45-90 prism. B) A model of a two-prism periscope

hits the next surface at an angle of 45 degrees. At
angles greater than 42 degrees, all the light will be
reflected within the glass; none will escape. The
reflected light will then hit the other surface at 45
degrees and be reflected again. The light will
emerge from the prism going in a direction opposite the way it entered. By turning the prisms as
shown in Figure 28b, you can make a light beam
follow the same path it did when you used mirrors (Figure 27).

Now that you know how a periscope works,

you might like to build one of your own. You'll need some cardboard, wood scraps, glue, scissors, and a pair of mirrors or prisms. Draw a plan of your periscope first; then go ahead and build it. Don't be surprised if your design changes as you proceed. It's not uncommon for scientists to change their plans. Things that look fine on paper may turn out to be more difficult when you actually build them.

SHADOW SCIENCE

Whenever you or something else comes between a source of light and the ground or a wall, a shadow forms. Have you ever noticed how big your shadow is when you stand near a light in an otherwise dark room? Have you seen your shadow grow shorter throughout the morning and then lengthen again as afternoon wears on? Have you noticed the many shadows cast by a baseball player at a night game? Or the colored shadows that are so numerous during the holiday season at the end of the year?

Shadows are a never-ending source of amazement. Sometimes they're sharp; sometimes they're fuzzy. Sometimes a shadow has the shape of the object that cast it; sometimes the shadow's shape is very different from the object that cast it. As you can see, shadows are a source of the kinds of questions of which science is made. That's one reason why I like experiments with shadows, but mostly I like shadows because they're fun to watch and play with.

Things You'll Need

- high-intensity bulb or a clear bulb with a straight-line filament
- lamp to hold bulb that acts as a point of light
- room with white wall
- two streetlamps or porch lights
- three lamps and bulbs
- solid cube, cone, and cylinder
- red, green, and blue light bulbs
- wooden dowel (optional)
- small mirror

This picture was taken in Asmer, India, at noon on a
day in late June. Notice that the shadows of the man
and the car are beneath them and have almost no length.
You can see virtually the same thing if you live near
Miami, Florida, or in the southern tip of Texas.

Earth is not the only place where you'll
find shadows. Where are these shadows?
What is the source that casts them?

SHADOW SIZE For this experiment you'll need a light that is very small. It should be as close to a point of light as possible. A high-intensity lamp bulb or a clear bulb that has a straight filament works well. If you use a clear bulb, you can turn it so that the end of the filament looks like a point of light. Use that point of light to cast shadows.

Place the point of light near one side of a room opposite a large, light-colored wall. Hold your hand close to the bulb, and look at the huge shadow of your hand on the wall. Slowly move your hand away from the bulb and toward the wall. What happens to the size of the shadow of your hand as you move closer to the wall? Using Figure 29 to help you, can you explain why the size of the shadow of your hand grows smaller as you move your hand away from the light?

MULTIPLE SHADOWS If you stand midway between two streetlamps at night, how many shadows do you cast on the ground? How do the lengths of the shadows compare? Which lamp is responsible for each shadow? Take a few steps toward one of the streetlamps. Which shadow grows longer? Which shadow grows shorter? Which shadow grows fainter? Which shadow grows darker?

Remove the shades from *two* room lamps. Place them about a foot apart near one side of a room opposite a large, light-colored wall. Now hold your hand in front of the two lamps and near the light-colored wall. How many shadows of your hand do you see? Suppose you had three lamps side by side. How many shadows of your hand would you expect to see?

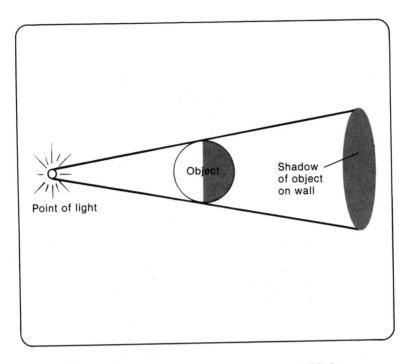

Figure 29. An object placed near a small light casts a shadow. What happens to the size of the shadow if the object is moved closer to the light? Farther from the light?

SHARP AND FUZZY SHADOWS Replace one of the lamps you used to cast two shadows with the small "point" of light you used before. If, with both lights on, you hold your hand near the wall, how many shadows of your hand do you expect to see? Try it! Were you right? But what's different about the two shadows? Which light do you think is causing the sharp shadow? Which light do you think is causing the fuzzy shadow?

To check up on your predictions, turn out the

small point of light. Which shadow disappears? Were your predictions correct? Why do you think one light casts a sharper shadow than the other? Would you expect the shadows cast by a fluorescent lamp to be sharp, or fuzzy? Why?

SHADOW SHAPES For this experiment you'll need three solid objects—a cube, a cone, and a cylinder. You'll also need a small point of light like the one you've used before. Look at the shapes of the shadows shown in Figure 30. All of the shadows can be made by holding at least one of the solid

Figure 30. How can you make the shadows shown in "a" with the three objects shown in "b"?

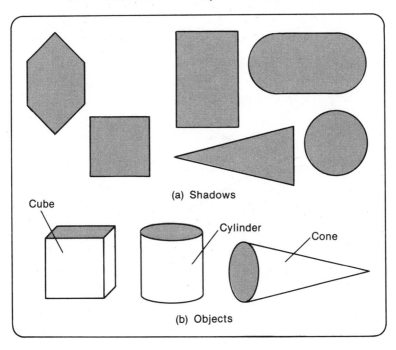

(a) Shadows

Cube

Cylinder

Cone

(b) Objects

objects in front of the small light. Predict which object you can use to cast each shadow; then test your prediction. Were you able to make all the shadows? Do you see now why some shadows don't look like the objects that cast them?

COLORED SHADOWS You can buy red, green, and blue light bulbs in a supermarket or hardware store. Place a green light bulb in one lamp. Place a red bulb in a similar lamp. Put the lamps side by side on a table in a room several yards or meters from a white wall. Hold your hand or a wooden dowel near the wall. How many shadows of your hand or the dowel do you expect to see? How many do you see? Notice that one shadow is green. What is the color of the second shadow?

Repeat the experiment using a red bulb and a blue bulb. How many shadows of your hand or dowel do you expect to see when you hold your hand or the dowel near the wall? What color do you expect the shadows to be? What color are the shadows? Were you right?

Predict the color of the shadows you will see if you use blue and green bulbs. Were you right?

Now use three lamps with red, green, and blue bulbs. Move your hand closer to and farther from the wall. What are the colors in the shadows you see? To see why you get shadows with colors you may not have expected, use a mirror to reflect some light from a green bulb onto some red light. What color do you get from this combination? How about a combination of red and blue light? Blue and green light? Now can you explain the colored shadows you saw when all three colored bulbs were used?

LOOKING AT THE MOON

Making observations of the night sky does not constitute an experiment *per se*. It can, however, help you to understand the changing positions of the moon and the planets, and give a sense of wonder at the vastness of space. When you look at the moon through a telescope or a good pair of binoculars, try to view it as Galileo might have. Galileo was probably the first person to see a magnified image of the moon through a telescope. Until he turned his telescope on the moon in about the year 1610, everyone believed that the moon and all other heavenly bodies were perfectly smooth spheres moving in perfect circles about the Earth. So before you look, expect to see a bright sphere with a surface smoother than a billiard ball. Only in that way can you appreciate Galileo's surprise.

If you continue to look at and watch for the moon over several months, you'll come to understand why the moon changes as it does each month, why it can often be seen in the daytime, and why it cannot be seen for a day or two each month. Once you understand the moon's cycle, you'll begin to look for it on a daily basis and you'll seek to understand why its rising and setting positions and time change from day to day, month to month, and season to season.

Things You'll Need

- small telescope or good pair of binoculars
- notebook
- newspaper

Use a small telescope or a good pair of binoculars to look at the moon. If possible, look when it is a new crescent moon, visible in the west shortly after sunset. Then try to look at it as often as possible from day to day until it is an old crescent moon rising just ahead of the sun in the morning. **Never look directly at the sun.**

How do you think Galileo felt when he saw an enlarged view of the moon? Can you see the long shadows cast by sunlight falling on the mountains of the moon? Can you see the giant craters that cover the moon's surface?

As you look at the magnified moon through its various phases from new moon to old moon, take note of some other things as well. In a notebook, record your observations about the moon each day that it's clear enough for you to see it. At what time does the moon rise each day? At what time does it set? (You can find this information in the newspaper if you happen to be in bed when the moon rises or sets.) Where does it rise and set? Where is the moon at various times of the day? You can give its position by its direction (north, south, east, west) and its altitude. Its altitude can be measured in degrees above the horizon. If you extend your arm straight out so that the top of your fist is level with the horizon, each fist that you add to the extended one as you go up toward the moon is equal to about 10 degrees. You'll find it takes just about nine fists to reach a point directly overhead.

What happens to the shape of the moon as time passes? Where is the moon with respect to the sun as the moon's shape changes? For example, when a full moon is rising, where is the sun? What happens to the angle between the sun and the moon as the moon waxes (grows bigger) and wanes (grows smaller)?

Watch the moon go through its cycle for several months. After you've collected all your information, see if you can offer an explanation of why the moon changes as it does.

Probably the easiest constellation to find is the
Big Dipper. It's made up of seven bright stars that
really do form the outline of a big water dipper or
cooking pan. See Figure 31. In the early evening it
can be found near the northern horizon in the fall
and early winter and high in the northern sky in
the spring and early summer. The pointer stars,
Dubhe and Merak, form an imaginary line that
points almost directly to the North Star (Polaris).
If you put your index finger and thumb on Dubhe
and Merak and move them along the line indi-
cated by these pointer stars, you'll find Polaris at
a point about five times the distance between
Dubhe and Merak. Polaris is not a brilliant star. It's
about as bright as Merak, and it is the end star in
the handle of the Little Dipper. Again, see Figure
31. The altitude of Polaris, which you can approx-
imate in fists, is always equal to the latitude
where you view it. On Cape Cod, where I live, the
North Star is always a little less than 42 degrees
above the horizon.

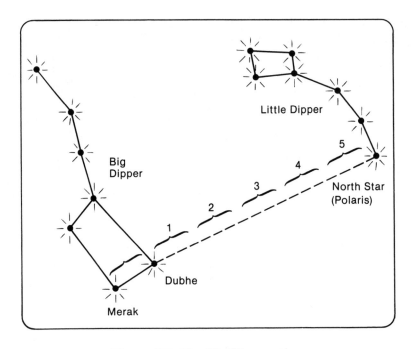

Figure 31. The Big Dipper, the
North Star (Polaris), and the Little Dipper

Once you've found Polaris, the Big Dipper, and
the Little Dipper, it's not hard to find the other
major northern constellations. The nice thing
about these constellations is that they are visible
all year long, which is not true of other constellations. Figure 32*a* shows you what these other constellations look like. Cassiopeia, which resembles
a dentist's chair, and Cepheus, which looks like a
pentagon, lie on the other side of Polaris from the
Big Dipper. If the Big Dipper is high in the sky,
these two constellations will be low in the sky
and vice versa. Draco (the Dragon) wanders across
much of the northern sky. Its tail lies between the

Star trails wheel around Polaris, the North Star,
in this 20-minute time-exposure photo.

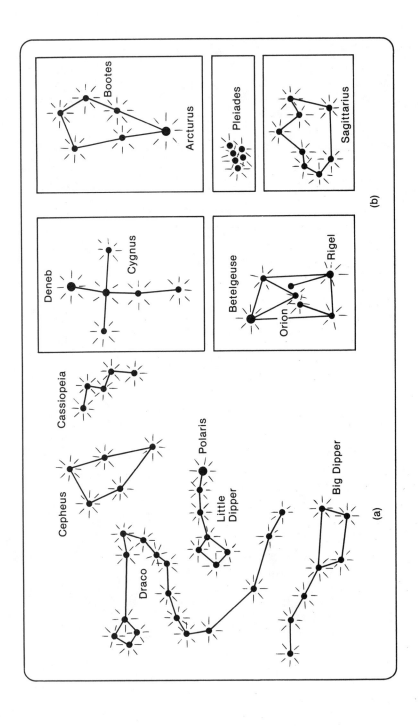

Big and Little Dippers and its head lies between the Big Dipper and Cepheus.

Figure 32b shows a few other bright constellations that can be seen during only part of the year. During the winter months, Orion the hunter can be identified quite easily. It rises earlier and earlier in the east as the winter progresses. Three bright stars in a line make up Orion's belt, which is easy to find. Betelgeuse (beetle juice) and Rigel are two bright stars above and below the belt, respectively. With a little imagination, you may be able to see the arms and legs of the hunter as well as his belt. To the east of Orion you may notice a constellation consisting of a cluster of seven stars that form a small dipper, much smaller than the Little Dipper. This constellation is known as the Pleiades or the Seven Sisters.

In the summer, the bright star Deneb can be seen at the top of the cross-shaped constellation, Cygnus (the swan), in the northern sky. Another bright star, Arcturus, forms the bottom end of the kite-shaped constellation, Boötes. In the southern sky you can see the constellation Sagittarius, which looks like the outline of an old coffeepot.

Figure 32. A) Some of the Polar constellations that rotate around the North Star (Polaris). B) Some other constellations

SUN AND SHADOWS IN SEASON

You know from experience that the sun is higher in the sky in summer than it is in winter. In this experiment you'll plot the sun's altitude, in degrees, at different times of the day and year. And you'll measure the largest and smallest midday altitudes of the sun.

All this can be done without ever having to look at the sun. By measuring the shadow of a stick, you can determine the sun's altitude. From your own experience, you know that your shadow is longest just after sunrise and just before sunset, when the sun is lowest in the sky. At midday, when the sun is high in the sky, your shadow is shorter. In fact, if you live on Neeker Island in the Hawaiian Islands, your shadow will be directly under you on about the 20th of June each year. Your shadow, like the shadow of the man shown in the photograph on page 85, will have no length because the sun will be directly overhead at midday.

Things You'll Need

- piece of plywood 3 ft × 3 ft
- thin wooden dowel 6 in long
- ruler or yardstick
- glue
- drill, and bit that matches the dowel's diameter (optional)

As you know, **you should never look directly at the sun.** In this experiment you won't have to. You'll be able to measure the sun's altitude from the length of the shadow of a stick.

Ask an adult to help you build the altitude-measuring instrument shown in Figure 33. It consists of a flat board 3 feet on a side and a thin dowel *exactly* 6 inches tall that is glued to the board near the midpoint of one side. The adult working with you may want to drill a hole to hold the dowel. That's fine so long as the dowel rises exactly 6 inches above the board. Use a T-square to be sure that the stick is perpendicular to the board.

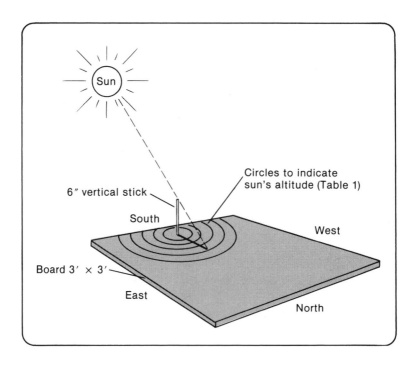

Figure 33. Measuring the sun's altitude
from the length of a shadow

Find a level place on the south side of your house where you can place the instrument. You should use a carpenter's level to be sure the board is level. By measuring the length of the stick's shadow and using Table 1, you can determine the altitude of the sun at any time it casts a shadow of the stick. Measurements for angles less than 10 degrees will not be very accurate and the shadow cast when the sun is less than 20 degrees above the horizon may extend beyond the board. Most of your measurements, however, will be reasonably accurate.

Table 1 Shadow lengths of a 6-inch stick converted to the sun's altitude

Sun's Altitude in degrees	Length of Shadow in inches	Sun's Altitude in degrees	Length of Shadow in inches
5	68$\frac{1}{2}$	50	5
10	34	55	4$\frac{1}{4}$
15	22$\frac{3}{8}$	60	3$\frac{1}{2}$
20	16$\frac{1}{2}$	65	2$\frac{3}{4}$
25	12$\frac{7}{8}$	70	2$\frac{1}{4}$
30	10$\frac{3}{8}$	75	1$\frac{5}{8}$
35	8$\frac{1}{2}$	80	1
40	7$\frac{1}{8}$	85	$\frac{1}{2}$
45	6	90	0

As you can see from the table, the shadow shrinks as the sun ascends higher in the sky. You may want to draw circles on the board with radii equal to the lengths of the shadows that indicate the sun's altitudes in the table. For example, a shadow that ended on a circle with a radius of 6 inches would mean that the sun's altitude was 45 degrees. A shadow whose end fell on a circle with a radius of 3$\frac{1}{2}$ inches would mean that the sun was 60 degrees above the horizon. The circles will make it easier for you to estimate the sun's altitude when the shadow's length lies *between* two values in the table.

Record the sun's altitude at different times during the day. Then plot a graph of altitude versus time. Such a graph made from information gathered at latitude 42 degrees on March 20 is shown in Figure 34. Try to plot similar graphs from information collected with your instrument

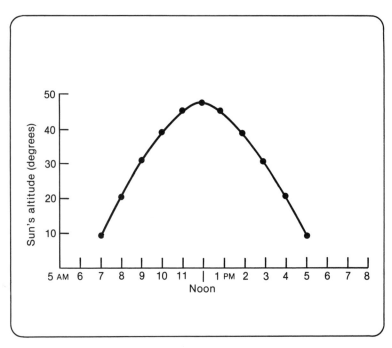

Figure 34. A graph of the sun's altitude vs. time at latitude 42° on March 20. At about what time did the sun rise? At about what time did it set?

for a number of days throughout the year. Try especially hard to collect such information for days on or about June 20 and December 20. How are your graphs similar? How do they differ?

In what direction does the shadow "point" when it is shortest? From your stargazing experiments you can find the North Star. If you do this with your instrument for measuring the sun's altitude in place, you will be able to mark the directions (N, E, S, and W) on the instrument.

From all the information you have collected,

plot a graph of the sun's maximum altitude versus the day of the year. At what time of the year does the sun reach its maximum altitude in the sky? At what time of the year is its maximum altitude lowest?

5

EXPERIMENTS WITH HEAT AND ELECTRICITY AND THE ART AND SCIENCE OF ESTIMATING

This final chapter presents a smorgasboard of experiments, several of which require a high degree of inventiveness and ingenuity on your part.

There are experiments on such yet-to-be covered topics as

- heat
- electricity
- soil science

In addition, I hope you'll enjoy learning how to make estimates; it's one of the most important things you'll ever learn. Being able to make reasonable estimates can save you a lot of time because estimates can show proposed courses of action to be fruitless. Furthermore, most of the things we plan cannot be worked out to the nearest second, inch, or ounce. Generally, we need to know something to the nearest hour, mile, or pound.

OERSTED'S DISCOVERY

With a little background information, this experiment allows you to share in the excitement of a discovery made by Hans Christian Oersted in 1819. For years before Oersted's discovery, scientists had thought there was no connection between electricity and magnetism. They knew that electric charges of the same sign (+ and + or − and −) repelled each other while charges of opposite sign (+ and −) attracted each other. They knew too that like magnetic poles (north and north or south and south) repelled one another while unlike poles (north and south) attracted each another. But electric charges and magnets had no effect on each other. Try to place yourself in that historical setting before you repeat the *accident* that led to Oersted's discovery.

Things You'll Need

- magnetic compass
- small magnet
- wire stripper
- insulated copper wire
- 6-volt dry-cell battery

When a wire is connected to the opposite (+ and −) poles of a battery, charges move through the wire from one pole to the other. Possibly charges have to be in motion before they produce any magnetic effect. That possibility was explored with great enthusiasm after Oersted's discovery.

Take a magnetic compass outside and hold it level in your hand. In which direction does the compass needle point? If you move to a different position, you'll see that the compass needle still points in the same direction.

Now take the compass inside and place it on a wooden table. There should be no steel or iron objects nearby because they may be magnets them-

A ship's compass. What determines the
direction in which the compass needle points?

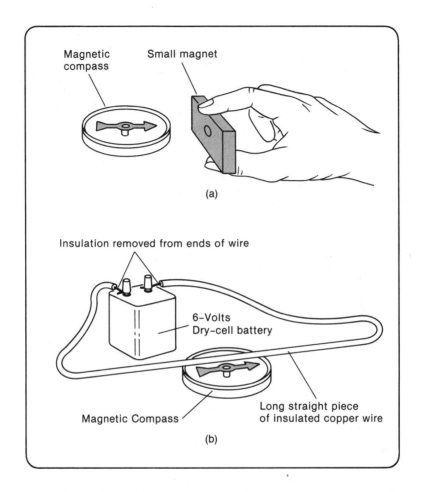

Figure 35. A) Bring a small magnet near a magnetic compass. What happens? B) What happens to the compass needle when electric charge flows in the wire?

selves. Move a small magnet toward the compass as shown in Figure 35a. (Don't get it too close or it might reverse the polarity of the compass needle.) You'll see that the compass needle is either attracted or repelled by the magnet. Now turn the magnet around and move it toward the compass needle again. What happens this time?

Now that you know how a compass needle is affected by the presence of something magnetic, you're ready to repeat Oersted's accidental discovery. Put the compass in the middle of the table as before. Use a wire stripper to remove about an inch of insulation from the ends of a long piece of straight, insulated copper wire. Then place the wire over the magnetic compass as shown in Figure 35b. Notice that the wire is above and parallel to the compass needle.

Now touch the ends of the wire to the opposite poles of a 6-volt dry-cell battery. (*Don't leave the wire connected for more than a few seconds.* It will wear down the battery very quickly.) What happens to the compass needle when electricity flows through the wire? Do you see why Oersted was so surprised when he did this by accident? What evidence did he have that electricity and magnetism are related?

Of course, others probably saw this same effect and paid no attention. A good scientist, like Hans Christian Oersted, notices things that *shouldn't* happen with more interest than those that should happen.

Repeat the experiment, but this time place the wire beneath the compass. In which direction does the compass needle turn this time? What happens if you repeat the experiment with the battery turned around so that the connections of the wire to the battery are reversed? Which way does the compass needle move this time?

You've seen that a magnetic compass needle moves when electric charge flows near it. You can use that principle to detect the flow of electric charges. Such a charge flow is called an electric current. To see if charge flows from the electric cell you'll build, you need a current detector—a galvanometer. You can make one by wrapping about 100 turns of enamel-coated copper wire around a folded H-shaped piece of cardboard that supports a magnetic compass. See Figure 36. Be sure to wind all 100 turns of wire in the same direction.

The enamel that coats the wire acts as an insulator preventing charge from "leaking" from one wire to another one next to it. The more turns you wrap around the compass, the smaller the current it can detect. Because the cell you're going to build will not produce much current, you've used

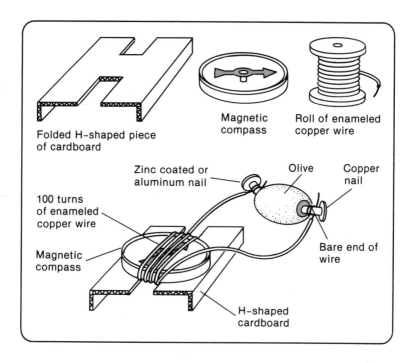

Figure 36. Building a galvanometer to test an electric cell you can eat

100 turns. You might need more. Use sandpaper to remove the last inch or so of enamel from each end of the wire. You need bare wire to make good contact between the wire and the poles of your electric cell.

To test your galvanometer, *briefly* touch the two bare ends of the enameled wire to the opposite poles of a 1.5-volt flashlight cell. The compass needle should whirl about rapidly when contact is made.

If your galvanometer is working, you can use it

to test your homemade electric cell. A pimento-stuffed olive or a hot pepper will serve as the electrolyte for your cell. A copper nail and a zinc coated or aluminum nail can serve as the two poles of your cell. They should both touch the pimento part of the olive, but *not* each other. Before you hold the wires against the nails, be sure the magnetic compass is level and the needle is parallel to the wire loops and free to turn. Now touch the two bare ends of wire to the two nails as shown in Figure 36. Watch the compass needle carefully. Does it move? What evidence do you have that charge is flowing in the wire?

Can you detect a current if you use a copper nail and an iron nail as the poles of your cell? Can you detect a current if you use two nails made of the *same* metal? Can you substitute another fruit, such as a lemon, for the olive or hot pepper and still detect a current?

ICE AND INSULATION

Normally when we talk about insulation, we are thinking of ways to keep heat from escaping from a warm house to the cold air outside. Or of a cup that keeps hot coffee or cocoa from cooling too fast or burning our hands. But insulation can also be used to keep heat from moving into a cold region. Refrigerators and freezers, for example, are surrounded by insulation.

In this experiment, you'll use insulation to keep an ice cube from melting for as long as possible. The experiment uses ice cubes, which are easy to obtain, and an easily defined end point—the totally melted ice. By using different materials as insulators, you'll be able to find out which ones work best.

Things You'll Need

- possible insulators—newspaper, cloth, sand, Styrofoam, fiberglass, aluminum foil, sawdust
- identical containers—paper or plastic cups, or small boxes
- cups
- ice cubes
- water, cooking oil, and rubbing alcohol
- sponge
- saucer

The living space in most buildings is
surrounded by insulation. This photograph
shows insulation being placed in a ceiling.

Before electricity and refrigerators, people
kept things cold by putting them in an icebox. An
icebox resembled a refrigerator. A large block of
ice was placed inside to keep the interior cold.

During the winter, people cut large blocks of ice from the surface of frozen lakes and ponds. The ice was stored in ice houses where it was surrounded by sawdust. In the spring, summer, and fall, people could come to ice houses and buy the blocks of ice that had been placed there during the previous winter. In some places icemen delivered ice door-to-door throughout the year.

Since ice was stored in sawdust, it seems likely that sawdust is a good insulator. If you don't have sawdust, you might use pencil shavings, which you can obtain from pencil sharpeners. In addition to sawdust, you might try newspaper, cloth, sand, Styrofoam, fiberglass, and aluminum foil.

Choose a set of identical containers such as paper or plastic cups, or small boxes. Fill each container nearly half full of an insulator to be tested. Put identical ice cubes in the containers and then fill the rest of each container with the insulation. The time it takes the ice cube to melt can be used to compare the insulating materials you are testing. Which of the materials you tested seems to be the best insulator?

Which do you think will be a better insulator, shredded paper or uncut paper? To find out, tear one sheet of newspaper into shreds. Leave another sheet in one piece. Use both to surround an ice cube as before. In which paper does the ice cube melt first? Which is the better insulator?

Are liquids good insulators? Find out this way. Place an ice cube in a cup containing water. Place an identical ice cube in a cup with an equal amount of cooking oil, and another in a cup with the same amount of rubbing alcohol. At the start all the liquids should be at room temperature. Place another ice cube in a cup that contains only air. In which container does the ice melt first? Are liquids good insulators?

Place one ice cube on a sponge so that its meltwater will be absorbed. Place an identical ice cube in a saucer so that it will sit in its meltwater. In which case does the ice take longer to melt? Is meltwater a good insulator?

Many years ago, in an article entitled "Can You Make a Better Ice-cube Keeper," which appeared in *Nature and Science*, David Webster claimed to be the World Champion Ice-cube Keeper. He was able to keep an ordinary ice cube from melting for sixteen hours in a room at 70° F (21° C). Can you beat his record?

ICE CUBES AND ICE PANCAKES

This experiment illustrates a very widespread and important principle, one that you touched on earlier when you tested the effect of area on the rate at which seltzer reacts with water. The surface area of a substance has an effect on the rate at which something happens. It may be the rate at which sugar dissolves in water, the rate that heat is lost from a home, the rate that water evaporates from a reservoir, or the rate that a seltzer tablet reacts with water, which you did in Chapter 1.

The beauty of this experiment is that the melting rate of ice is slow enough to see, yet fast enough to be done in a reasonable period of time. Furthermore, it can be done with materials that almost anyone can find.

Things You'll Need

- plastic ice cube container or ice cube tray
- cover from a plastic container
- water
- freezer
- two sponges or saucers
- containers with different shapes—cone, cylinder, pyramid, etc.

Pour about an ounce of water, or enough to fill the container, into a plastic cube used to make ice cubes. If you don't have individual cubes, use one compartment of a plastic ice cube tray. Pour an equal volume of water into a shallow, circular cover from a plastic container. Place both containers in a freezer to make a cube of ice and a broad, flat pancake-shaped piece of ice.

After the water is thoroughly frozen, remove the pieces of ice from the freezer. Which piece of ice has more surface area; that is, which piece has more of the ice exposed to the air?

Place both pieces of ice on identical saucers or sponges. Which piece do you think will melt first? Which one does melt first? How does the amount of surface area affect the rate at which ice melts?

You may be able to find containers that would enable you to make a variety of ice shapes, all with the same volume. You might make a cone, a sphere (ball), a pyramid, and a cylinder, as well as a cube and a wide, flat cylinder (pancake). Of all the ice shapes you can make, which one do you think will melt the slowest? The fastest?

Use what you have learned about the effect of surface area on the melting rate of ice to answer the following questions. (You may want to test your answers by experiment.) Which do you think will dissolve faster in a cup of tea, a sugar cube or an equal amount of loose sugar? Which will evaporate faster, a glassful of water or the same amount of water poured on a sidewalk? Which will warm faster in sunlight, a can filled with water or the same amount of water in a wide pie pan?

The Mendenhall Glacier near Juneau, Alaska.
Taking into account what you have learned
about the various properties of ice, what
could you do to make a glacier melt faster?

SOILS AND WATER

To have a good garden you must have good soil. If the soil doesn't hold water, plants will dry up and die. If the soil doesn't allow water to drain slowly through it, seeds will rot. Where I live, the soil is very sandy. You'll see the problem with sandy soil in this experiment. Perhaps the soil where you live is just right for gardens. In any event, this experiment shows you how to test different soils to see how much water they can hold. It's an example of how scientific thinking can be applied to practical problems.

Things You'll Need

- several samples of soil
- large paper cups, two for each soil sample
- newspapers
- sharp pencil
- wooden coffee stirrers or pencils
- measuring cup
- water

Soil is made up of tiny pieces of material that was once rock or organic material such as grass or leaves. To see how much water different soils hold, you'll need to collect some soil samples. You can probably find sand, gravel, potting soil, humus, topsoil, clay, and whatever soil is in your garden.

For each soil, you'll need a large paper cup and a newspaper. Put about three quarters of a cup of each type of soil you have collected on a newspaper. Then spread the soil out so it can dry. Leave the soils in a warm, dry place for about a week to be certain they are thoroughly dry.

Use a sharp pencil to punch some holes in the bottom of each paper cup. Then put the dried soils into the cups. On the side of each cup, write the type of soil it contains. Place each cup on top of another cup as shown in Figure 37. You can use wooden coffee stirrers or pencils to support the cups of soil.

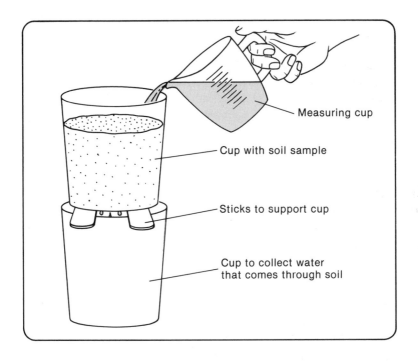

Figure 37. How much water do different soil samples absorb?

Fill a measuring cup to the 1-cup line with water. Slowly pour the water onto the soil until it begins to run out the holes in the bottom of the cup. Let the excess water drip through into the lower cup. Once the dripping stops, pour the water back into the measuring cup. How much water did this soil sample absorb?

Repeat the experiment for each soil sample. Which soil can hold the most water? What is the problem with sandy soil? Are there any soils that you think might hold too much water? Which kind of soil makes the best mud pies?

THE ART AND SCIENCE OF ESTIMATING

Almost everyday I read something in the paper that I know is not true. I know it's false because I can make a reasonable estimate of what it should be. For example, a local paper reported that the town budget for next year would be $650,000. Now I know that the public library's budget is nearly $100,000, which is only 1.4 percent of the total town budget. So as a rough estimate, let's say the library gets 1 percent of the budget. Then the total budget must be about 100 times the amount that goes to the library. That's 100 × $100,000 or $10,000,000. I'm sure that the article meant to say $6,500,000, but someone mistakenly moved the decimal point one space to the left making the number $650,000.

Suppose I wanted to paint my house. The first thing I'd do is estimate the total area to be painted. Then I'd find out how much area a gallon of paint will cover (it's printed on the can). Now if a gallon of paint will cover 300 square feet, and the area to paint is about 2,000 square feet, I need to buy about 6 gallons. I might need 7, but there are windows and doors that occupy some of the area so 6 is probably about right.

Most of the estimates I make are simple. How much time must I spend in the library to do the reading I need to do? How much will the groceries cost? How much gasoline will I use on a trip to Maine? There's no end to making estimates. Keep track of how many you make in a day. The number will surprise you.

The first estimate you'll be asked to make may seem impossible at first. But don't give up! Follow the procedure described and you'll see its quite easy to do. Once you've made the first estimate, you'll have the confidence you need to do others.

Things You'll Need

- grassy area—lawn, park or playground
- ruler
- yardstick or measuring tape
- box of rice
- measuring cup

Estimate the number of blades of grass in your lawn. "Impossible!" you say. But actually it's quite easy. Choose a region of your lawn where the growth of grass is about average. Measure off a square inch (an area 1 in × 1 in) and count the number of blades of grass in that small area. Let's say you count 20 blades. Now use a yardstick or measuring tape to find the entire area of your lawn. Suppose it's 150 feet by 200 feet. That's an area of 30,000 square feet (150 ft × 200 ft). In each square foot there are 144 square inches (12 in × 12 in). In 30,000 square feet there are 4,320,000 square inches (144 × 30,000). In each square inch there are about 20 blades of grass. Therefore, an estimate of the number of blades of grass in the lawn would be 20 × 4,320,000 or 86,400,000 blades of grass in the entire lawn. An estimate of 50,000,000 to 100,000,000 is close enough.

Now go ahead and estimate the number of blades of grass in your lawn or a section of a park or playground. How many blades do you estimate there are? Before you made this estimate, you knew only that the number was large. But you wouldn't have known whether it was closer to a million or a billion.

Here's another estimate you can make. How many grains of rice are there in a box of rice? To make this estimate, pour the rice into a measuring cup until it reaches the 1-ounce level. Then count the grains in the cup. You now know about how many grains there are in 1 ounce of rice. If you measure the total volume of the rice in the box, how can you estimate the total number of rice grains?

Now that you have some experience in making estimates, here are some other estimates to make. (If you have some estimates of your own that you'd prefer to make, do those instead.)

Make estimates of:

- The number of words in this book.
- The number of books in your school's library.
- The volume of water that you drink each year. Would it fill a bathtub? Would it fill a swimming pool?
- The number of chocolate chips in a box of chocolate chip cookies.
- The number of leaves on a tree.
- The number of hairs on a friend's head.
- The number of people in a theater. At a ball game.
- The number of hot dogs eaten each year in the United States.

You've probably seen big jars of beans where you're asked to guess the number of beans in the jar. How would you go about making a reasonable estimate of the number of beans in the jar?

For Further Reading

Gardner, Robert. *Energy Projects for Young Scientists*. New York: Franklin Watts, 1987.

————. *Experimenting with Illusions*. New York: Franklin Watts, 1990.

————. *Experimenting with Inventions*. New York: Franklin Watts, 1990.

————. *Experimenting with Light*. New York: Franklin Watts, 1991.

————. *Experimenting with Sound*. New York: Franklin Watts: 1991.

————. *Famous Experiments You Can Do*. New York: Franklin Watts, 1990.

————. *Ideas for Science Projects*. New York: Franklin Watts, 1986.

————. *Kitchen Chemistry*. New York: Messner, 1988.

————. *More Ideas for Science Projects*. New York: Franklin Watts, 1989.

————. *Projects in Space Science*. New York: Messner, 1988.

————. *Science Around the House*. New York: Messner, 1985.

————. *Science Experiments*. New York: Franklin Watts, 1988.

Gardner, Robert, and Webster, David. *Moving Right Along*. New York: Doubleday, 1978.

———. *Science in Your Backyard*. New York: Messner, 1987.

———. *Shadow Science*. New York: Doubleday, 1976.

Webster, David. *Exploring Nature Around the Year: Fall*. New York: Messner, 1989.

———. *Exploring Nature Around the Year: Spring*. New York: Messner, 1990.

———. *Exploring Nature Around the Year: Summer*. New York: Messner, 1990.

———. *Exploring Nature Around the Year: Winter*. New York: Messner, 1989.

———. *Towers*. Garden City, N.Y.: Natural History Press, 1971.

INDEX